eat drink live

eat drink live

150 RECIPES FOR MORNING NOON NIGHT

FRAN WARDE

PHOTOGRAPHY BY DEBI TRELOAR

RYLAND
PETERS
& SMALL

LONDON NEW YORK

Senior Designer	Louise Leffler	
Food Editor	Elsa Petersen-Schepelern	
Editors	Maddalena Bastianelli	
	Jenni Muir	
Index	Hilary Bird	
Production	Patricia Harrington	
Location Researcher	Kate Brunt	
Art Director	Gabriella Le Grazie	
Publishing Director	Alison Starling	
Food Stylist	Fran Warde	
Food Stylist's Assistant	Janet Dalzel Piper	
Stylists	Emily Chalmers	
	Abigail Aherne	
	Karina Garrick	
Photographer's Assistants	Lina Ikse Bergman	
	Brian Benson	

First published in Great Britain in 2000
by Ryland Peters & Small
20–21 Jockey's Fields, London WC1R 4BW
www.rylandpeters.com

This paperback edition first published in 2005

10 9 8 7 6 5 4 3 2

Text © Fran Warde 2000
Design and photographs © Ryland Peters & Small 2000

Printed and bound in China

ISBN 978 1 84172 825 4

A CIP record for this book is available from the British Library.

notes

All spoon measurements are level unless otherwise stated.

All fruits and vegetables used in this book should be washed thoroughly and peeled in the usual way, unless otherwise advised.
Carrots in particular should be peeled, topped and tailed, and apples
and pears should be cored before juicing. Unwaxed citrus fruits and
cucumbers should be used whenever possible. Remember that pregnant women, very young children, plus the infirm and elderly, should
avoid eating raw eggs and soft or blue cheeses.

eat drink live **contents**

introduction

Cooking is a joy and eating is a pleasure, so my kitchen is a happy sanctuary. From the age of two I was allowed to cook at home. OK, I can hear Mum calling me an 'assistant mess maker', chucking flour here and there, pouring half the sugar in the bowl and the other half on the worktop, squeezing butter through my fingers, but it was fun and certainly much better than playing in sand as all the textures were different and we could eat what we made.

Gardening was also important in my family and just about everything was home grown. My summers were spent picking peas and shelling them, gathering runner beans and slicing them with a very old-fashioned slicer, cutting lettuces and washing them, digging and peeling carrots. I would sit amongst the strawberries and raspberries, pluck them straight from the plant and pop them into my eager little mouth. We climbed apple, pear and plum trees, gathering the plumpest fruits which we would share with our donkey and my guinea pigs. It was fun but also the start of my appreciation of good fresh food. We would watch it grow, then gather it to cook and serve at the table for a comforting family meal. I loved it.

I hope that I have the same patience as my Mum had with me when it comes to teaching my two boys this most wonderful of basic life skills. We all need to eat, and the best food is home-cooked and made from good fresh produce.

What started in my formative years as play time and a game has continued to follow me through life. Catering college beckoned, then off I went to the Café Royal in London, all bright eyed and bushy tailed, I left 18 months later feeling

You must be able to laugh in your kitchen and share the triumphs, as well as those moments when you do not achieve perfection, with ease and happiness. Cooking should be one of life's pleasures. We all need food to thrive, and the better the food the better we live. It is a joy to eat a freshly cooked meal, prepared with thought, consumed with an enjoyable drink and taken in good company.

very sad and despondent, so I decided to take another tack. First I cooked my way around the UK and Mediterranean, then the other side of the world beckoned and off I went. It was fantastic. I landed in Australia with just £300, which was not a lot even 15 years ago. My Australian friends were kind but I needed to work. Luckily the fusion food trend was beginning there and I was intrigued, excited and fascinated – all my senses exploded. The time spent in Australia was hugely important to my culinary education and my brain was working overtime storing and gleaning information.

One of the craziest things I have ever done was to set off to sea one night on a small fishing boat out of Darwin, with four guys I had only just met. I had always wanted to see fish at its best, so that later in life I could say with authority 'That is not fresh!' It was the best and worst eight days of my life. I was scared and couldn't find my sea legs, but the fish, prawns and crayfish were fantastic and I got to swim with dolphins. It was the most informative fish course that I have ever been on. Learning all about fish and how to store and fillet them from a fisherman is a privilege and I had no need to be scared. I eventually found my sea legs and went back to sea for another three weeks!

When I returned to London I just cooked and cooked. Ideas were falling out of my head and the adrenalin was whizzing around my body. While working as a caterer I was offered an exciting opportunity to open a restaurant with a friend. We had a small fixed menu as well as a large roving menu that changed according to the produce available and what we felt like cooking.

I loved cooking in the restaurant: orders pouring in, temperatures rising, working as a team, customers waiting, praise being given, pots being washed, the kitchen being cleaned and tomorrow's menu being planned for it all to start again. I thrived on it but eventually left and moved into writing and teaching.

As you will see from this book, my food is eclectic and gathered from all over the world. It's very hard to say exactly what my style of cooking is, but I think of it as enjoyable to prepare and delicious to eat. You must be able to laugh in your kitchen and share the triumphs, as well as those moments when you do not achieve perfection, with ease and happiness. My basic principles of good cooking are as follows:

Go shopping and choose what is fresh, seasonal and looks so good that you simply have to buy it. That may be because of its colour, smell, texture or simply a yearning you have to handle and taste it.

Cook with passion, pleasure, kindness and interest. When preparing your feast, keep it simple and don't hesitate to stay within your abilities – if you over-stretch and stress yourself in the kitchen you will only become frustrated. Cooking should be one of life's pleasures. We all need food to thrive, and the better the food we eat, the better we live.

The final essential part of good cooking is the eating. It is a joy to eat freshly cooked food, prepared with thought, consumed with an enjoyable drink and taken in good company. This will always be one of life's most important and sociable skills, therefore I say: 'Eat Drink Live.'

menu planner

v – suitable for vegetarians

Vegetarian and Vegetable Dishes

V Artichoke and Cheese Tart, 146
V Baked Aubergines with Pesto Sauce, 60
V Blue Cheese and Rosemary Polenta
    Mash, 119
V Braised Red Cabbage, 83
V Creamy Mustard Mash, 83
V Curried Lentils and Spinach, 119
V Ginger Asparagus with Cashew
    Nuts, 166
V Minted Beans and Peas, 83
V Potatoes Boulangère, 153
V Ratatouille, 76
V Roasted Vegetables, 83
V Sautéed Vegetables in Shallot Butter, 168
V Tomato and Goats' Cheese Tart, 93
V Vegetable Couscous, 75

Rice, Noodles and Pasta

Chicken and Tarragon Pesto Pasta, 54
Crab Spaghetti with Chilli Mussels, 44
V Crusted Golden Rice Bake, 161
V Lemon Spaghetti, 112
V Mushroom Risotto, 121
Paella, 134
V Risotto Primavera, 122
Spaghetti Bolognese, 116
Spaghetti Carbonara, 129
V Spaghetti Puttanesca, 116
V Thai Meatballs and Noodles, 133
Thai Noodle Salad, 113
V Vegetable Noodle Stir-fry, 133

Meat, Poultry and Fish Dishes

Baked and Glazed Ham, 153
Chicken and Chestnuts with Lentils, 167
Chicken and Vegetable Satay Sticks, 90
Chinese Duck Breast, 174
Couscous with Roasted Chicken and
    Vegetables, 115
Green Chicken Curry, 151
Lamb with Rosemary and Garlic, 80
Middle Eastern Barbecue Lamb, 159
Peppered Beef and Watercress, 146
Roast Pork with Sage and Apple, 79
Rosemary and Lemon Roasted
    Chicken, 58
Steamed Sea Bass with Thai Soup, 167
Salmon Fishcakes, 152
Steak and Mushroom Pie, 125

Puddings and Desserts

V Banoffi Pie, 126
V Chilled Lemon Soufflés, 168
V Chocolate Pudding Cake with
    Raspberries, 84
V Damper with Red Berry Salad, 48
V Espresso Granita, 64
V Honey and Pistachio Panna Cotta, 162
V Lemon Meringue Pie, 84
V Lemon Tart, 75
V Nectarine Tart, 63
V Nutty Toffee Apples and Toffee
    Cherries, 56
V Pears with Star Anise and Chocolate
    Drizzle, 177
V Plum Clafoutis, 168
V Quick French Apple Tart, 154
V Steamed Syrup Pudding, 134
V Tarte Tatin, 126
V Tiramisu, 148
V Upside-Down Pear Cake, 77
V Watermelon Granita, 155
V Watermelon and Rosewater Salad, 162

Baking

V Banana Bread, 27
V Celebration Iced Fruit Cake, 108
V Coconut Jam Biscuits, 109
V Coffee and Walnut Cake, 27
V Cranberry and Orange Muffins, 21
V Flapjacks, 27
V Lemon Syrup Cake, 108
V Mini Chocolate Brownie Squares, 64
V Plum Pastries, 21
V Soda Bread, 103
V Spiced Muffins, 32
V Sultana Scones, 105
V Strawberry Tarts, 107

Preserves, Dressings and Sauces

V Classic Tomato Sauce for Pasta, 117
V Delicious Vinaigrette, 61
V Hollandaise Sauce, 153
V Preserved Lemon and Tomato
    Pickle, 161
V Pesto Sauce, 60

Alcoholic Drinks

V Blueberry Martini, 137
V Brazen Martini, 137
V Cosmopolitan, 138
V French 75, 138
V Kick-Starter Bloody Mary, 29
V Lobby Dazzler, 142
V Mojito, 141
V Mulled Wine, 151
V Pimm's Cocktail, 138
V Sea Breeze, 138
V White Wine Spritzer, 50

Non-Alcoholic Drinks

V Banana Smoothie, 99
V Breakfast Blitz, 17
V Café Frappe, 38
V Iced Jasmine Tea, 107
V Lemon and Ginger Infusion, 107
V Still Ginger Lemonade, 53
V Melon and Strawberry Juice, 22
V Super Juice, 22

morning

I love my bed, so breakfast has to be really good to entice me to start the day. During the week, wake me with a mug of steaming fresh coffee and a bowl of granola. But give me a lazy weekend and I want to ease myself into the day with an indulgent yet civilized breakfast of fresh juices and fruits, sizzling bacon, poached eggs, thickly cut toast with melting butter and jam, muffins, tea and newspapers to read slowly. Make time this weekend for yourself, celebrate breakfast and feel fantastic. Then, when life needs a mid-morning sweetener, try freshly baked banana bread, irresistible flapjacks or coffee and walnut cake with tea or coffee, the height of comfort food. Share an elegant brunch with friends and family and serve a spicy Bloody Mary and luscious kedgeree with poached eggs, or panettone French toast with cinnamon and hot bananas. Relax and lounge the morning away, slowly eating and talking — pure bliss.

quick and healthy breakfasts   tea know-how   Sunday morning celebration

coffee know-how   something sweet.....with coffee   weekend brunch

quick and healthy breakfasts

Breakfast is an important meal, but there never seems to be enough time to enjoy it. Everyone – including me – would rather spend longer in bed. However, you should try to make time for breakfast as it will set you up for the rest of the day. Prepare one of these quick and easy dishes to make sure your first meal of the day is delicious and nutritious.

Plum and apricot compote

Eat lots of fruit every day as part of a healthy diet. Make a batch of fruit compote, then store it in the fridge ready to serve every morning with a bowl of granola or muesli. You can cook this compote on top of the stove or bake it in the oven. I prefer the latter because the fruit seems to hold its shape better.

If you like spices, stir ½ teaspoon mixed spice, ground cinnamon or freshly grated nutmeg into the compote before cooking. Vanilla essence or the grated zest of an orange or lemon is also delicious.

500 g plums, halved and pitted
500 g apricots, halved and pitted
125 g light brown sugar
Serves 4

Put the prepared fruit in an ovenproof dish, sprinkle with the sugar, then add 200 ml water. Cover and cook in a preheated oven at 180°C (350°F) Gas 4 for 30 minutes until the fruit is tender and the juice is syrupy.

House granola

After tasting this you will forget all other granolas and feel virtuous knowing that you really did make your own breakfast. Store the cereal in an airtight container for up to 4 weeks – if it lasts that long.

300 g rolled oats
50 g whole almonds
50 g raisins
25 g ready-to-eat dried apricots
25 g pumpkin seeds
25 g golden caster sugar
4 tablespoons maple syrup

a non-stick baking sheet
Serves 4

Mix all the ingredients together in a large bowl, then transfer to the baking sheet. Bake in a preheated oven at 160°C (325°F) Gas 3 for 25 minutes until toasted.

Remove from the oven and stir well. Return the mixture to the oven and cook for a further 15 minutes until the granola is crisp and light golden.

Remove the cereal from the oven. Eat while hot with milk, or let cool, then transfer to an airtight container and store.

Breakfast blitz

This drink is pure nutritional heaven. Thanks to the growing popularity of vegetable juices, juice extractors are becoming more affordable and soon every keen cook and healthy eater will own one. Make sure you buy organic produce for juicing; it is important not to peel the vegetables and fruit as key vitamins are stored just below the skin.

2 apples, cored
2 beetroot, trimmed
2 carrots, trimmed
2 celery stalks
2.5 cm fresh ginger, peeled
Serves 4

Put the fruit and vegetables into the juicer and extract the juice according to the manufacturer's instructions. Pour into glasses and serve immediately.

Boiled egg and soldiers

This deliciously simple breakfast is a winner every time. The trick is to serve the egg perfectly cooked, with thick strips of hot buttered toast (known as 'soldiers') for dunking.

4 free-range eggs, at room temperature
4 slices bread
unsalted butter, for spreading
sea salt and freshly ground black pepper
Serves 4

Fill a small saucepan with water and heat until barely simmering. Lower the eggs, on a spoon, into the water and let them simmer for 3–4 minutes for soft-boiled, 5–6 minutes for medium-cooked or 8–9 minutes for hard-boiled eggs.

Meanwhile, toast the bread, spread with butter and cut into 4–5 strips or soldiers. Serve with the eggs and small piles of sea salt and freshly ground black pepper. To eat, dip the soldiers into the egg – just perfect!

top tip: To avoid cracked shells, use eggs that are at room temperature and gently lower them on a spoon into barely simmering water. Simmer rather than boil and don't let them jostle around in the pan.

Growing, harvesting and roasting

Tea leaves come from an Asian evergreen shrub that grows abundantly in China, India, Sri Lanka, Japan, Indonesia, East Africa, Latin America and Russia. Good growing conditions are essential to the fine flavour of a tea. The plants favour a hot, humid climate with warm winters that are not too dry. Most important however is the altitude, which should be about 2000 metres above sea level to produce a fine and fragrant tea with good colour.

Tea is an every-hour, everyday drink in the West, whereas in China and Japan it forms an important part of cultural life and the tea ceremony features as part of social customs and traditions. When it first arrived in Europe, tea was primarily associated with the aristocracy, but once it became more readily available, it was popular at every level of society.

Teas are classified according to the quality of leaves picked from the shrub; the younger the leaves, the better the tea. Broken larger leaves are used in lesser teas. Leaves are treated in different ways to make various types of tea:

Green tea is unfermented but roasted immediately after harvesting to give a clear infusion with a delicate taste. It is popular in China and Japan. Varieties include Gunpowder, Gen Mai Cha, Lung Ching and Sencha. Just a little pinch is needed to make a cup of green tea, otherwise the flavour will be too strong.

Black tea is fermented and dried, giving an infusion with a strong taste and rich amber colour. It is the most common type of tea and there are many different varieties to choose from, including Assam, Darjeeling, Lapsang Souchong and Superior Orange Pekoe. Go to a tea shop in your area and taste some samples: the differences are really quite amazing.

Oolong tea is a semi-fermented leaf that is fragrant with a sweet aftertaste. Grown in Taiwan and very popular in America, there are eight grades ranging from choicest to common. Try Fancy Grade Oolong, which gives a mellow infusion best drunk without milk.

Scented tea comes in many varieties, the most famous of which is Earl Grey, a black tea with oil of bergamot added. Other scented teas may have flowers, fruit, leaves, stems or roots added to create the fragrance.

Herbal teas are also called tisanes because they do not contain any real tea leaves. There are many varieties, including camomile, jasmine, lemongrass, peppermint and raspberry, and they can be drunk hot or cold.

Stored in a dark place, tea can be kept for a year. I think it is important to have a lovely teapot that pours well. Some people will only drink tea out of china mugs or cups – this is for you to choose. In my view, tea is all too often made in a mug, which is fine for green tea and herbals, but black and oolong teas really require the space of a teapot to brew properly.

Making black, oolong or scented tea

Always use freshly boiled filtered water. Rinse out the teapot with the boiled water, then add the tea, allowing 1 teaspoon per person and one for the pot. Pour in the boiled water and leave to infuse for 3–5 minutes. Do not over-infuse the tea or it will become bitter and dark.

How strong and what to add, if anything, is a matter of personal taste. Tea can be drunk black, or with a dash of cold milk; some people take sugar and others a slice of lemon. I like it very weak and black, a simple, pure infusion.

Making green and herbal tea

These can be made in a mug for one person but if you are making for any more, use a teapot. Green tea is best weak so calculate ½ teaspoon of tea per person, and the same for herbal. Many herbal teas come in individual bags and one of these per person is the best ratio. Brew for 1 minute – no longer or it will become bitter, then drink without milk or sugar.

potted perfection
tea

Sunday morning celebration

Lazy weekend breakfasts are so good. I love that special feeling when time seems to stand still and the fast – often chaotic – pace of weekday life slows right down. Why not start the day with a cup of tea or coffee in bed to gently wake you from your slumber, then head to the kitchen to create one of these extra-special breakfasts?

Swiss muesli

This soft muesli is steeped overnight in creamy yoghurt, then served topped with delicious summer berries and honey.

200 g rolled oats
75 g bran flakes
75 g dried apple pieces
75 g raisins
75 g desiccated coconut
75 g chopped toasted hazelnuts
25 g sunflower seeds
450 ml plain yoghurt

To serve

500 g mixed fresh berries, such as
    blueberries, raspberries and strawberries
4 tablespoons honey
Serves 4

Mix all the dry ingredients in a large bowl. Add the yoghurt, mix well, cover and chill overnight.

Serve in bowls with a scattering of berries and the honey drizzled over the top.

Plum pastries

Fill these easy pastries with your favourite fruit and nuts. Croissant dough, found in the chiller cabinets at large supermarkets, freezes well, so you can make freshly baked pastries any time you want.

1 can chilled ready-to-bake croissant dough,
    about 250 g
6 plums, halved and pitted
4 teaspoons honey
1 tablespoon flaked almonds

a baking sheet, lightly oiled
Makes 6

Remove the dough from the can, unravel it and flatten. Cut along the perforations to make 6 rectangles and lay well apart on the baking sheet.

Put 2 halves of fruit on each piece of pastry, then drizzle with honey and sprinkle with the almonds.

Bake in a preheated oven at 180°C (350°F) Gas 4 for 15–20 minutes until puffed and golden. Remove from the oven and serve hot or cold.

Cranberry and orange muffins

I can hear you shouting: 'Who has time to make these?!' But I can assure you they don't take long. Send the family out for a jog or to walk the dog and, while they're away, turn on the radio and get baking. They'll thank you for these fruity muffins.

200 g self-raising flour
225 g caster sugar
1 teaspoon cinnamon
2 oranges
250 ml sour cream
50 g butter, softened
1 egg, lightly beaten
150 g cranberries

a 12-hole deep muffin tin, lined with
    8 muffin paper cases
Makes 8

Sift the flour into a bowl, then stir in the sugar and cinnamon.

Grate the zest from the oranges and reserve. Slice off the white pith, then cut down between the membranes to release the segments.

In a second bowl, beat the sour cream with the butter, egg and orange zest until smooth. Add to the dry ingredients and mix gently.

Add the cranberries and orange segments and fold gently into the mixture using as few strokes as possible. Do not beat or overmix; the batter should look slightly streaky.

Spoon the mixture into the prepared muffin cases, filling each one to about two-thirds full.

Bake in a preheated oven at 180°C (350°F) Gas 4 for 35 minutes until golden and firm to the touch. Remove from the oven and eat warm with butter and a cup of coffee or tea.

top tip: To check if the muffins are cooked, insert a skewer, cocktail stick or the tip of a pointed knife into the centre of one muffin: it should come out clean. If not, continue baking for 5 more minutes.

'The works'

An indulgent breakfast unlike traditional fried versions. It is cooked primarily in the oven and packed with flavour, not grease.

4 top-quality sausages
4 medium open-cap mushrooms
4 slices smoked back bacon
2 large tomatoes, halved
2 tablespoons vegetable oil
4 free-range eggs
4 slices wholemeal or wholegrain bread
butter, for spreading

a large baking sheet, lightly oiled
Serves 4

Arrange the sausages and mushrooms on the baking sheet, spaced well apart, and cook in a preheated oven at 180°C (350°F) Gas 4 for 15 minutes. Turn the sausages and mushrooms, add the bacon and tomatoes, return to the oven and cook for a further 15 minutes.

Heat the oil in a non-stick frying pan, add the eggs, then cover and cook for 2 minutes, or until the surface of the eggs becomes opaque.

Meanwhile, toast the bread and spread with butter. To serve, put the toast on 4 heated plates, top with the eggs and add the sausages, bacon, mushrooms and tomatoes.

Smoked salmon bagels with poached eggs

Here is a light alternative to a fried breakfast – and it is so easy to make. For me, smoked salmon and poached eggs are truly delicious and a real luxury. Treat yourself to this wonderful breakfast or, better still, get your partner to make it for you.

4 bagels
butter, for spreading
100 g watercress or rocket
200 g smoked salmon
4 eggs
sea salt and freshly ground black pepper
a bunch of chives, to serve
Serves 4

Cut the bagels in half, toast them, then lightly spread with butter. Top with watercress or rocket, folds of salmon and a twist or two of black pepper.

Crack the eggs into 4 cups. Bring a large saucepan of water to the boil and, when simmering, stir the water around in one direction to create a whirlpool. Gently slip each egg into the water, return to a gentle simmer and cover with a lid. Remove the saucepan from the heat and let stand for 6 minutes.

Remove the eggs with a slotted spoon and drain on folded kitchen paper. To serve, put the eggs on top of the bagels, then add the chives.

For a change, try scrambled eggs. Put 5 eggs, 5 tablespoons milk and a pinch of salt in a bowl and beat with a fork. Heat 25 g of butter in a non-stick frying pan, pour in the egg mixture and stir with a wooden spoon until the eggs are almost set to a soft, creamy scramble. To serve, spoon the eggs on top of the prepared prepared bagels.

Melon and strawberry juice

These summer fruits, now available all year round, make a delicious, refreshing drink. Juice them for breakfast or to have instead of tea.

1 melon, such as cantaloupe or honeydew
1 punnet strawberries, about 200 g, hulled
juice of 2 limes
8 ice cubes, plus extra to serve
Serves 4

Chop the melon flesh into small pieces and put in a blender with the berries, lime juice and ice. Blend until smooth and serve in a large chilled jug.

top tip: For a flavoured yoghurt drink, add natural yoghurt to the blender with the fruit.

Super juice

A pure, clean-tasting drink for a special breakfast treat.

1 medium pineapple or 400 g canned pineapple
   chunks in natural juice
3 large bananas, sliced
200 ml cranberry juice
8 ice cubes
Serves 4

If using fresh pineapple, top and tail it, cut away the skin and remove all the dark prickly spots. Cut the pineapple into quarters lengthways, then remove the core from each section. Chop the fruit and put into a large jug.

Add the bananas, cranberry juice and ice, then whizz with a hand-held blender until there are no lumps. Serve in chilled glasses.

coffee

the coffee knowledge

Growing, harvesting and roasting

Coffee plants grow in sub-tropical climates around the world. Its fruit looks similar to cherries but over 6-9 months will ripen to a very dark brown. Each 'cherry' contains two coffee beans which are removed by drying, soaking or husking of the cherry flesh. The beans are then sorted and bagged to be transported.

At their final destination, the beans are roasted. Roasting caramelizes the sugars and carbohydrates in the bean and produces that distinctive aroma and flavour we all love. How the beans are roasted will effect the flavour of the coffee. Dark roasted beans have a rather sharp, acidic flavour that is good for espresso, whereas lightly roasted beans have less caffeine and acidity and are best used in cafetières or filters.

Blending and grinding

Blending is a complex art, but also a matter of taste. If you go to a specialist coffee merchant, they will make a blend to suit your very own personal taste – experiment with different brands and blends and beans from different parts of the world until you find the perfect cup for your household.

The beans are ground according to the method you use to make your coffee: use coarsely ground coffee for a percolator, medium grind for a drip filter or cafetière and fine grind for espresso machines. For really good, fresh coffee, try to grind your own beans – the flavour is much richer. Keep the beans in an airtight container in the fridge. If you must buy your coffee ready-ground, buy only what you need for the week and store it in the refrigerator.

Making coffee

As a rough guide, use 2 level tablespoons of freshly ground coffee per cup if using a cafetière, drip filter or espresso machine. Rinse the cafetière out with hot water, add the coffee and fill with hot water. Leave to steep for 3 minutes then gently plunge. Follow the manufacturer's directions for espresso machines. If you prefer white coffee, serve it with scalded milk for a real treat.

something sweet.....with coffee

Banana bread

I discovered this amazing cake in a coffee bar in Queenstown, New Zealand. It was so good that I had to have a second piece.

250 g butter, softened
225 g golden caster sugar
2 eggs, lightly beaten
2 large bananas, mashed, about 225 g
375 g self-raising flour, sifted
75 ml milk
1 teaspoon vanilla essence

a 1 kg loaf tin, greased and lined
Serves 8

Cream the butter and sugar in a bowl until light and creamy, then add the beaten eggs, a little at a time, mixing well between each addition.

Mix in the mashed banana and fold in the flour. Add the milk and vanilla and mix until smooth.

Pour into the loaf tin and bake in a preheated oven at 180°C (350°F) Gas 4 for 50 minutes.

Let cool in the tin for 10 minutes, then turn out onto a wire rack to cool completely.

Flapjacks

Who can resist these sweet, sticky treats? They are easy and fun to make, so get your children to help too. For a fruit and nut variation, add sultanas or raisins and some chopped pecans, walnuts or hazelnuts to the mixture before baking.

250 g butter, softened
200 g golden syrup
150 g demerara sugar
400 g rolled oats

a shallow cake tin, 30 x 20 cm, lightly greased
Makes 12

Put the butter, syrup and sugar in a saucepan and melt over a low heat, mixing well.

Add the oats and stir until evenly coated.

Tip the mixture into the prepared cake tin. Using a round-bladed knife, push the mixture into the corners of the tin and roughly level the surface.

Bake in a preheated oven at 200°C (400°F) Gas 6 for 15 minutes, until golden brown.

Remove from the oven, cool for 5 minutes, then cut into squares or rectangles. Let cool in the tin for a further 10 minutes.

Remove from the tin and serve with tea or coffee.

Coffee and walnut cake

No coffee break is complete without some cake to recharge energy levels. A slice of this will keep you going until lunchtime.

250 g butter, softened
250 g caster sugar
4 eggs, lightly beaten
5 teaspoons instant coffee granules
250 g self-raising flour, sifted
100 g walnut halves

Coffee buttercream

100 g butter, softened
300 g icing sugar, sifted, plus extra
    for dusting
3 teaspoons instant coffee granules

2 sandwich tins, 15 cm diameter, lightly greased
    and base-lined
Serves 4–6

Put the butter and sugar in a bowl and, using a wooden spoon or electric beater, beat until pale and creamy. Beat in the eggs, a little at a time, until the mixture is light and fluffy.

Dissolve the coffee in 5 tablespoons hot water, then stir into the butter and egg mixture. Using a large metal spoon, fold in the flour.

Divide the mixture evenly between the sandwich tins and level the surface. Bake in a preheated oven at 180°C (350°F) Gas 4 for 20–25 minutes until the cake is golden and a skewer inserted in the middle comes out clean. If it doesn't, bake for a further 5–10 minutes, then test again. Remove from the oven.

Let cool in the tins for 5 minutes, then turn out onto a wire rack to cool completely.

To make the coffee buttercream, put the butter and icing sugar in a bowl and beat until smooth and fluffy. Dissolve the coffee in 2 tablespoons hot water and mix into the buttercream.

To assemble the cake, lightly dust a plate with icing sugar and put one of the cakes on the plate. Spread it with half the buttercream and top with the other cake. Spread the remaining buttercream on top and make a pattern in it with a fork. Decorate with the walnut halves. This cake is best eaten the day it is made.

top tip: To prevent the cake mixture from curdling when beating in the eggs, add a tablespoon of the flour after each addition of egg.

When you need an energy boost, something sweet and home-made is best, so never let your cookie or cake tin sit empty. These recipes will inspire you to start baking and fill the larder with mid-morning treats that are just as delicious mid-afternoon.

weekend brunch

Brunch is a wonderful way to entertain. The day is still young and it is the weekend, so everyone has a great lounging feeling. Mix a few drinks, get in the newspapers and chat about the week's happenings while you slowly eat your way into the day.

Kick-starter Bloody Mary

If you or your guests can't face alcohol so
early in the day, it is a good idea to make
two jugs of this drink – one with everything
and the other without the vodka.

5 lemons
200 ml vodka
7 cm white horseradish, freshly grated, or
   1 tablespoon bottled horseradish
1 tablespoon Worcestershire sauce
1 teaspoon Tabasco sauce
lots of freshly ground black pepper
750 ml tomato juice, well chilled
celery stalks, with leaves, to serve
Serves 4

Half fill a large jug with crushed ice. Cut one of
the lemons into slices and squeeze the juice
from the others. Add to the jug, together with all
the other ingredients except the celery. Mix well.
Serve in highball glasses with a celery stalk.

menu

Kick-starter Bloody Mary

Fruit platter

Spiced muffins

Kedgeree with poached egg

Panettone French toast with
cinnamon and bananas

Café frappé

Fruit platter

Everyone loves fruit, especially if it's all
been prepared for them and looks stunning.
This one is always a brunch winner.

1 ripe melon, such as orange cantaloupe
   or green honeydew
2 papayas
juice of 2 limes
300 g mixed berries, such as blackberries,
   blueberries, raspberries, redcurrants
   and strawberries

Honey yoghurt
450 ml plain yoghurt, preferably Greek
6 tablespoons clear honey
Serves 4

Peel, halve and deseed the melon, then cut into
wedges and slice. Divide between 4 plates. Peel,
halve, deseed and cut the papaya into wedges.
Add to the melon. Sprinkle with lime juice, then
add the berries.

Put the yoghurt in a bowl, drizzle with the honey
and serve with the fruit.

Spiced muffins

These easy-to-make muffins are packed with aromatic spices. Chopped fruit keeps them deliciously moist while the maple syrup adds a smoky, sticky sweetness.

250 g self-raising flour, sifted
175 g soft brown sugar
1/4 teaspoon ground cinnamon
1/4 teaspoon freshly grated nutmeg
100 ml milk
1 egg, lightly beaten
3 tablespoons peanut oil
1 apple, cored and chopped, about 175 g
2 bananas, chopped, about 200 g
10 teaspoons maple syrup

a 12-hole deep muffin tin, lined with
    10 paper cases
Makes 10

Mix the flour, sugar, cinnamon and nutmeg in a large bowl, then make a well in the centre.

Mix the milk, egg and oil in a small bowl or jug, then pour into the well you have made in the dry ingredients. Stir quickly with a wooden spoon until mixed, being careful not to overmix.

Fold in the chopped apple and bananas, then spoon the mixture into the prepared paper cases, filling each one to about two-thirds full.

Make a hollow in the top of the muffins with the back of a teaspoon and add 1 teaspoon maple syrup to each one – don't worry if it drizzles out.

Bake in a preheated oven at 180°C (350°F) Gas 4 for 20 minutes. Remove from the oven and serve immediately, or cool on a wire rack.

top tip: Cooking the muffins in pretty paper cases prevents the mixture sticking to the tin and helps each muffin keep its shape. It also makes them look special for your guests.

Invite your friends over at the weekend for a relaxing brunch and give them a feast. I always think brunch should be served on Sundays so that you can calmly prepare for it the day before. Buy fresh fruit and groceries from the market and gather brightly coloured flowers – this is all part of the fun.

To add a touch of style to your brunch party, lay the table with your best white, tablecloth and use your lovely china, cutlery and glasses. Float flower petals in a glass bowl filled with water or stand large sculptured-looking flowers, such as lilies, in a tall vase. Finally, to create a relaxed atmosphere and stylish setting, remember to keep everything simple, clean and natural.

Kedgeree with poached eggs

For fish lovers everywhere, this simple and yet scrumptious recipe will be extremely satisfying. Smoked haddock is the traditional fish for kedgeree, but you should stay away from any smoked haddock that has been artificially dyed to a bright yellow colour.

375 g undyed smoked haddock
150 g long grain rice
200 g baby spinach, trimmed and washed
4 large eggs
grated zest and juice of 1 lemon
60 g butter
a bunch of chives, chopped
sea salt and freshly ground black pepper

an ovenproof dish, lightly buttered
Serves 4

Put the haddock in the ovenproof dish in a single layer, skin side down, and cover with foil. Cook in a preheated oven at 180°C (350°F) Gas 4 for about 10 minutes. Remove from the oven and let cool a little. When cool enough to handle, flake the fish and carefully remove and discard any bones and skin.

Put the rice in a saucepan and add enough water to cover the rice by 2 cm. Bring to the boil, then cover and simmer for 12 minutes. (Do not remove the lid during cooking.) Let stand for a few minutes before removing the lid, then stir in the spinach and cook for 1 minute. Drain well.

To poach the eggs, crack the 4 eggs into 4 cups. Bring a large saucepan of water to the boil and, when simmering, stir the water in one direction to create a whirlpool. Gently slip each egg into the water, return to a gentle simmer, then cover, remove from the heat and let stand for 6–7 minutes, depending on how cooked you like the yolks.

Meanwhile, gently mix the poached haddock flakes with the rice, lemon zest and juice, butter, salt and pepper. Spoon the mixture into a lightly buttered dish, cover and keep it warm.

Remove each egg from the pan with a slotted spoon. Use folded kitchen paper to absorb any excess water from under the spoon. Put the eggs on top of the kedgeree, sprinkle with the chives and serve.

top tip: If you don't like smoked haddock, use a mixture of fresh salmon and prawns instead. It makes a truly delicious alternative.

Panettone French toast with cinnamon and bananas

Panettone is a sweet, fruity bread from Italy, traditionally eaten at Christmas, but I think it's far too good to restrict to the festive season. Fortunately, you can now buy it all year round in Italian delicatessens.

4 eggs
3 tablespoons single cream
1 teaspoon ground cinnamon, plus extra for dusting
4 thick slices panettone
75 g butter
4 bananas
maple syrup, to serve
Serves 4

Beat the eggs, cream and cinnamon in a bowl with a fork, then pour into a shallow, flat-bottomed dish. Add the slices of panettone, let soak for 5 minutes, then turn them over and let soak on the other side for 5 minutes.

Heat the butter in a large, heavy, cast-iron or non-stick frying pan. When the butter is foaming, drain off the excess egg mixture from the panettone and add the soaked slices to the pan. Cook for 4–5 minutes on each side or until golden.

Put the cooked panettone on a heated serving plate and keep it warm in a low oven. Slice the bananas into the frying pan and toss gently for 5 minutes. Spoon them over the top of the panettone, then drizzle with the maple syrup and dust with cinnamon. Serve hot as soon as possible.

After brunch it's time to settle into a comfy chair and enjoy a sumptuous creamy coffee while flicking through the magazine section of the paper. Your contented guests can leave at their leisure, or stay on for more chatting, some wine or perhaps a trip to the pub via the local park. Leave the dishes as long as you like: we were not meant to work on Sundays.

Café frappé

A real treat – café frappé is very refreshing and makes a great change from regular coffee. I prefer this drink made with good instant coffee (to me it gives it a smoother flavour and velvety texture), but if you prefer real coffee, make it in the usual way and use 2 tablespoons for this recipe.

900 ml full-fat milk, chilled
100 ml double cream, chilled
2 tablespoons instant coffee granules
12 ice cubes

Serves 4

Mix the milk and cream in a jug or bowl, then put in the freezer for about 3 hours until frozen. Chill 4 glasses in the freezer until cold.

Put the instant coffee in a cup with 1 tablespoon boiling water. Stir to dissolve the granules, then cool and chill.

Put the frozen creamy milk, coffee and ice cubes in a blender and whizz until smooth.

Pour into the chilled glasses and serve at once.

If you don't like coffee, try making crushed tea. Simply make a pot of weak tea such as Earl Grey, jasmine, green tea or one of your favourites. Cool the tea and put it in the freezer. Fork through the tea every 20 minutes to break up the large ice crystals that form. When firm and icy, spoon the mixture into chilled glasses and top with sliced peaches or orange wedges. This also makes an exotic light pudding to finish off an indulgent meal.

top tip: To give your frappé a kick, add a dash or two of rich coffee liqueur such as Kahlúa – it's heaven, but for adults only.

noon

What a glorious time of day, with the sun high in the sky and lunch about to begin. This is my favourite meal, after a busy morning my tummy is yearning for food. The best lunches in my view are always those eaten on holiday or at weekends when the atmosphere is relaxed and indulgent and a long, slow meal with wine can gently drift into the afternoon. Lunch can be taken anywhere and in any style but the one necessity is time: it is very important to sit down and eat slowly, to talk with friends and enjoy yourself. Busy people often take lunch on the move or, as I like to say, on the hoof. This is not the most relaxing way to eat, but in modern society it is a fact of life. Please don't let your midday meal be a bag of crisps. With some planning and just a little bit of effort the night before, a great packed lunch that is fresh and healthy can be made to brighten your day and provide good nourishment.

beach barbecue family picnic garden lunch summer salads winter salads

winter lunch Saturday family lunch classic Sunday roast working lunch

food on the move snack attack teatime

Whisk me off to a sunny beach and I am happy, surrounded by friends, family, children playing and sand between my toes. I like to sip a white wine spritzer as I light the barbecue, have a dip in the sea while the coals are heating, then return to cook a delicious but easy lunch in the open air. A favourite choice is crab spaghetti and chilli mussels accompanied by a crisp salad and crunchy garlic toast drizzled with olive oil. Afterwards, we simply lie back and breathe in the happiness.

beach barbecue

Crab spaghetti with chilli mussels

This deliciously simple dish can be made on a barbecue or by building a safe fire. Don't forget to take two saucepans and a colander.

7 tablespoons olive oil
1 onion, chopped
2 garlic cloves, crushed and chopped
1 can chopped tomatoes, 400 g
1 glass white wine, about 150 ml
1 mild red chilli, deseeded and finely chopped
375 g dried spaghetti
400 g cleaned mussels
1 medium dressed crab
juice of 1 lemon
a bunch of flat leaf parsley, coarsely chopped
sea salt and freshly ground black pepper
Serves 4

Heat 4 tablespoons of the olive oil in a medium saucepan over the hot coals. Add the onion and garlic and cook until softened and translucent.

Add the chopped tomatoes, white wine, chopped chilli, salt and pepper. Mix well, bring to the boil and simmer for about 10 minutes to reduce and thicken the sauce.

Bring a large saucepan of water to the boil, add the spaghetti and push it down into the water. Stir to separate the strands and stop them sticking together. Cook for about 9 minutes, or until *al dente* (cooked, but 'firm to the tooth').

Meanwhile, discard any open mussels that will not close when tapped sharply with a knife. Add the mussels to the sauce, mix well, then cover with a lid and simmer for 4 minutes.

Drain the spaghetti into a colander. Add the remaining olive oil to the same pan, and gently stir in the crabmeat, lemon juice and chopped parsley. Add the drained spaghetti, return to the heat and toss well to mix all the ingredients.

Serve the spaghetti in piles with spoonfuls of chilli mussels and sauce on top.

top tip: Try to buy a dressed crab, readily available in supermarkets, food halls and from fishmongers by the sea. Cooking a fresh, raw crab is very simple, but extracting the meat can be a long, slow process. With a dressed crab the fiddly work is done for you, and it tastes much better than canned crab.

top tip: If any mussels remain unopened after cooking, it may be that there wasn't enough heat generated in the saucepan. Make sure the pan is boiling and covered. If any of the mussels still don't open, discard them.

Eating under the sun surrounded by nature is wonderful, but it is important to take all the necessary gear on a barbecue to enjoy your day fully. Make a list and double-check that you have all that's needed for the perfect day out. Don't throw the list away either: I promise this day will be so special that you will want to repeat it soon.

Lightly drizzle the garlic-flavoured bread with olive oil and sprinkle with sea salt before serving hot.

top tip: Try using different breads for garlic toast. It is delicious made with a loaf of farmhouse white, multigrain, soda or sourdough bread, not just baguette.

Summer salad

This quick and simple salad sparkles with the good, clean, peppery taste of watercress and the delicious crunch of radish and celery.

300 g watercress, ends trimmed
a bunch of radishes, trimmed and halved
6 celery stalks, sliced
4 tablespoons olive oil
2 tablespoons balsamic vinegar
sea salt and freshly ground black pepper
Serves 4

Put the watercress in a salad bowl, then add the halved radishes and sliced celery.

Drizzle with the olive oil. Add the vinegar and seasoning, toss well and enjoy.

top tip: Some salad items are not good travellers and by the time they make it from your shopping basket to the table, they may have seen better days. Replace any of the ingredients in the above salad with whatever is fresh and best in the market on the day: remember shopping should always be flexible.

Garlic toast

No one can resist thick slices of crunchy hot toast topped with garlic and extra virgin olive oil.

4 thick slices of your favourite bread
1 large garlic clove
extra virgin olive oil, to serve
sea salt
Serves 4

Toast the bread on each side. Rub one side of each piece with the peeled garlic clove, letting the toasted bread act as a grater and catching the small bits of garlic.

Damper with red berry salad

To me this is real summer outdoor cooking and eating. We used to make these sticks of bread endlessly as kids and dip them into big pots of home-made strawberry jam.

400 g seasonal red berries
50 g caster sugar
150 g self-raising flour
25 g butter, cut into small pieces
100 ml milk or water
double cream or clotted cream, to serve

8 wooden satay sticks, rubbed with butter at one end
Serves 4

Put half the berries in a medium bowl, add the half the sugar and coarsely crush the fruit with the back of a fork. Stir in the remaining berries and set aside.

Put the flour in a second medium bowl. Add the butter and use your fingers to rub it into the flour until the mixture is smooth. Add the remaining sugar and liquid and mix well until the mixture sticks together and forms a dough.

Divide the dough into 8 pieces and shape them into sausages around the end of the buttered sticks. Cook over the whitened embers of a barbecue or fire for approximately 15 minutes, turning constantly. When cooked they should be lightly coloured and firm.

Serve the damper on small plates with the crushed fruits spooned over and a dollop of whipped double cream or clotted cream alongside.

top tip: You can also cook the dough sticks on a greased baking sheet in the oven at 200°C (400°F) Gas 6 for 12-15 minutes.

White wine spritzer
A pretty spritzer to cool a hot brow.

1 bottle white wine, 750 ml, chilled
1 litre sparkling mineral water, chilled
400 g frozen white grapes
Serves 8

Put the chilled white wine, mineral water and frozen grapes in a large jug and mix well. Serve the spritzer in your favourite large glasses.

top tip: Frozen fruit cubes are great taken on picnics to chill drinks. They do not melt as quickly as ordinary ice cubes and children love eating them too. Try chopping up some orange segments, putting them in ice cube trays, adding fresh orange juice to cover, then freezing.

family picnic

When the weather is great, quickly gather some food and head to an open space to eat from your lap. Don't forget to take a book and a game or two so you can really make an afternoon of it. The menu here is perfect for a relaxed and enjoyable lunch.

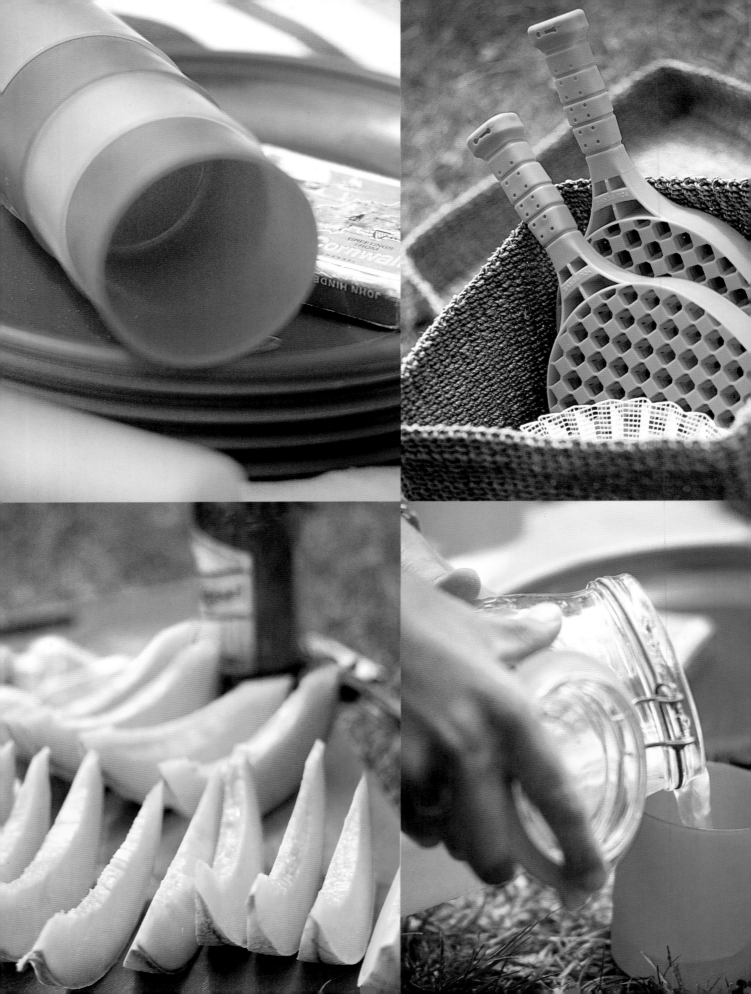

top tip: Always remember to take a chopping board and a sharp knife with you on a picnic – it's much better to slice bread on arrival for real freshness, and these pizzas are best when they travel whole.

menu

Still ginger lemonade

Toasted ciabatta pizzas

Chicken and tarragon pesto pasta

Nutty toffee apples and toffee cherries

Still ginger lemonade
It is worth making a weekly batch of this drink as it is so refreshing and there is something rather satisfying about being served a good home-made lemonade.

10 cm fresh ginger, peeled and very finely sliced
juice of 4 lemons
1 lemon, sliced
75 g sugar
Serves 4

Put the ginger, lemon juice, sliced lemon and sugar in a heatproof jug and pour on 1 litre boiling water. Mix well and let steep for 2 hours. Chill, then serve poured over crushed ice.

top tip: Many variations can be made on this drink. If you don't like lemons, use limes or oranges and, for a really clean taste, add mint. If you want something stronger, add a shot of vodka to each glass.

Toasted ciabatta pizzas
Other breads can be used in these fantastic, fresh-tasting pizzas, so don't go shopping specially for ciabatta. You can also use Cheddar or blue cheese instead of mozzarella.

1 loaf ciabatta, split lengthways or sliced
1 garlic clove, peeled
about 4 tablespoons olive oil
4 ripe tomatoes, skinned and sliced
a handful of pitted olives
a bunch of marjoram
2 balls mozzarella cheese
a bunch of basil
sea salt and freshly ground black pepper
Serves 4

Grill the ciabatta under a hot grill until lightly toasted, then rub with the garlic, using it like a grater. Put the garlic ciabatta on a baking sheet and drizzle with a little of the olive oil.

Arrange the sliced tomatoes on the bread, then add the olives, marjoram, mozzarella, basil, salt and pepper. Drizzle more oil over the top.

Cook in a preheated oven at 180°C (350°F) Gas 4 for 15–20 minutes until the tomatoes are softened and crisp round the edges and the mozzarella has melted. Remove, let cool and wrap in parchment paper before packing.

Chicken and tarragon pesto pasta

This really is a great dish – tarragon and chicken go together so well. Kids will love it, yet it tastes good enough for adults to tuck into as well. Pesto can be made out of most herbs, so don't hesitate to try your favourites in this recipe and blend to create your own version. We eat a lot of this one at home: it's scrumptious.

300 g dried penne pasta
9 tablespoons olive oil
75 g Parmesan cheese, freshly grated
75 g pan-toasted pine nuts
a large bunch of tarragon, leaves stripped from
  the stem and chopped
grated zest and juice of 1 lemon
1 garlic clove, crushed and chopped
3 cooked chicken breasts, sliced
100 g rocket
sea salt and freshly ground black pepper
Serves 4

Bring a large saucepan of water to the boil. Add the pasta, stir and cook for 8–9 minutes, until *al dente* ('firm to the tooth'). When cooked, drain and refresh the pasta in cold water, then drain thoroughly and toss in 4 tablespoons of the oil.

Put the Parmesan, pine nuts, tarragon, lemon zest and juice, garlic and remaining oil in a jug and purée until smooth with a hand-held blender.

Put the pasta, pesto, chicken and rocket in a serving bowl, season and toss well, coating the pasta and chicken evenly with the pesto.

top tip: If you don't want meat, replace the chicken with steamed vegetables such as courgettes, sugarsnap peas, broad beans or runner beans.

top tip: When taking this salad on a picnic, don't add the rocket until just before eating or the oil will make it wilt.

For sophisticated parkland grazing, supplement your cooking with wedges of juicy fresh melon, salty slivers of prosciutto crudo, chunks of piquant salami or chorizo, some mouthwatering olives, an oozy cheese and some crunchy hazelnut biscotti. Pack in a crate for easy transport and don't forget the beer.

Nutty toffee apples and toffee cherries

Your dentist won't be happy with this recipe but I can assure you that you will be.

400 g sugar
20 cherries, with stalks
4 apples
100 g chopped nuts
Serves 4

Put the sugar in a small saucepan with 200 ml water and bring to the boil. Reduce the heat and simmer until golden. Do not use a spoon to stir the mixture, just swirl the pan: this keeps the heat even and stops the sugar from crystallizing.

When the caramel is golden, remove the pan from the heat. Holding the stems, quickly dip the cherries into the hot caramel, then put them on a sheet of baking parchment to set.

Spear the apples onto forks. Add the nuts to the caramel and heat through briefly if it is too stiff. Dip the apples in the mixture, swirling them around until coated all over with the nutty caramel. Put on the baking parchment to set for about 5 minutes. Do not let the apples or cherries touch each other or they will stick together.

Wrap the apples and cherries separately in sheets of baking parchment to take to the picnic.

When the weather is good, I can't resist eating outside and, for a special celebration, it's such fun to do it in grand style. Pull the table into the garden and bring out the chairs. Decorate with pretty napkins, flowers and foliage, candles – don't stop. For maximum conviviality, put all the food out for friends and family to help themselves, then settle down to eat, drink and soak up the atmosphere.

garden lunch

Rosemary and lemon roasted chicken

In a simple dish such as this, quality ingredients are important. Choose an organic or free-range chicken, unwaxed lemons, a good Modena balsamic vinegar and extra virgin oil. It really makes a difference.

about 2 kg chicken pieces, or 1 whole chicken*
3 lemons, cut into wedges
leaves from a large bunch of rosemary
3 red onions
75 g large black olives, about 10–12, pitted
4 tablespoons balsamic vinegar
2 tablespoons extra virgin olive oil
sea salt and freshly ground black pepper

Serves 4

Trim off any excess fat from the chicken pieces and put them in a large bowl. Add the lemon and rosemary.

Cut the onions in half lengthways, leaving the root end intact. Cut the halves into wedges and add to the chicken.

Add the olives, balsamic vinegar, olive oil and seasoning and mix well to coat the chicken with the flavourings.

Cover and let stand at room temperature for 1 hour, or in the refrigerator overnight.

Put the chicken in a large roasting tin, then add the marinade ingredients. Cook in a preheated oven at 190°C (375°F) Gas 5 for 30 minutes. Turn the chicken pieces thoroughly in the tin to ensure even cooking and colouring, then cook for a further 30 minutes.

Remove the chicken from the oven. Using a slotted spoon, lift out the chicken, lemon, onions and olives and put them on a serving dish.

Skim the cooking juices, discarding the fat. Pour the juices over the chicken and serve hot or at room temperature.

*Note: If using a whole chicken, lay the bird on its back. Use a large knife to cut through the skin between the leg and breast of the chicken, then bend the leg backwards until the joint cracks. Cut through the joint to separate the leg. Repeat on the other side.

Bend the drumsticks back away from the thighs to crack the joints, then cut through with the knife to separate. Bend back the wings of the chicken and cut through the joints near each breast to separate.

Put the bird on its side and use scissors or poultry shears to cut from the leg joint up along the backbone to the neck. Repeat along the other side. (Wrap the backbone and store for use in stock another day.)

Hold the chicken breast-side down and bend it back to crack the breastbone. Use the scissors to cut along each side of the breastbone and remove the breasts.

Chickpea, tomato and pepper salad

I have a passion for chickpeas, but have found that most people don't really know what to do with them. Using the canned variety, as in this super Mediterranean-style salad, makes it so easy.

5 plum tomatoes, halved and deseeded
3 large red peppers, halved and deseeded
375 g canned chickpeas, rinsed and drained
a bunch of flat leaf parsley
sea salt and freshly ground black pepper
extra virgin olive oil, to serve

Serves 4

Lightly oil a roasting tin and add the tomatoes and peppers. Cook in a preheated oven at 190°C (375°F) Gas 5 for 20 minutes.

Remove from the oven and transfer the tomatoes and peppers to a bowl. Add the drained chickpeas, then mix in the parsley and seasoning.

Transfer the salad to a serving dish, sprinkle with a little olive oil, then serve at room temperature.

Leaf and herb salad

This may be a simple salad, but simplicity is best when you're working with the fragrant flavours of herbs. To make it extra pretty, garnish with edible flowers such as heartsease, nasturtiums and pansies when available.

300 g mixed leaves or 1 head of lettuce
a handful of edible flowers (optional)

4 bunches of herbs, such as basil, chives, marjoram, flat leaf parsley, sage, tarragon, fennel and lovage
3–4 tablespoons Delicious Vinaigrette (page 61)

Serves 4

Wash and trim the mixed leaves or lettuce as necessary. Tear into a bowl. Add the edible flowers, if using, and a selection of your chosen herbs. Drizzle with the vinaigrette, toss well and serve immediately.

Let the sky be full of sun and your table full of delicious food. Laying all the dishes out at once is easy on the cook, but also a sure way to get the conversation and laughter flowing freely while guests help themselves and each other. Graze in leisurely fashion, nibbling happily as the day wears on and empty bottles of wine mount up.

Baked aubergines with pesto sauce

If you can find them, use the little Asian aubergines to make this dish – they look very pretty and have a more interesting texture than large aubergines. When buying herbs, try going to independent greengrocers or market stalls where they are sold in big bunches, like flowers – I find these herbs taste better and are much better value.

300 g small aubergines
4 tablespoons olive oil

Pesto
a large bunch of basil
75 g pan-toasted pine nuts
1 garlic clove
75 g Parmesan cheese, grated
6-8 tablespoons olive oil
sea salt and freshly ground black pepper

a baking sheet, lightly oiled
Serves 4

Cut the aubergines in half lengthways and put on the baking sheet. Drizzle with a little of the oil and bake in a preheated oven at 190°C (375°F) Gas 5 for 15-20 minutes, then turn them over and cook for a further 15 minutes.

To make the pesto, put the basil, pine nuts, garlic, Parmesan, the remaining olive oil and seasoning in a blender and purée until smooth. When the aubergines are cooked, drizzle with pesto and serve hot or cold.

top tip: Make twice the quantity of pesto and store the extra in the fridge – it always comes in handy as an easy salad dressing or tossed through pasta for a quick, delicious supper. Keep the pesto covered with a thin film of olive oil and it will stay fresh for several weeks.

Delicious vinaigrette

Making this vinaigrette with a hand-held blender gives such a thick texture that it clings to the salad leaves. Children love it – give them bread or vegetable sticks for dipping. Store any leftovers in an airtight bottle in a cool dark place (but not the fridge).

100 ml white wine vinegar
juice of ½ lemon
2 teaspoons Dijon mustard
2 teaspoons wholegrain mustard
1 teaspoon caster sugar
250 ml olive oil or vegetable oil
sea salt and freshly ground black pepper
Serves 4

Put the vinegar, lemon juice, Dijon and wholegrain mustards, sugar, salt and pepper in a jug. Whizz with a hand-held blender or whisk by hand.

While still blending, slowly pour in the oil. When it has all been incorporated, you will have a fantastic emulsion. If it seems too thick, just add a little water and blend again.

Nectarine tart

Crumbly sweet pastry and oozingly juicy nectarines make a sensational combination. The delicate summer flavours of white peaches and apricots make a lovely alternative filling for this tart. Come autumn, don't hesitate to use plums.

240 g plain flour
250 g butter, softened and cut into small pieces
100 g icing sugar, plus extra for dusting
2–3 egg yolks
1.25 kg nectarines or peaches
real vanilla ice cream, to serve

a 20 cm loose-based tart tin
Serves 6–8

Put the flour, butter and icing sugar in a food processor and whizz until the mixture looks like breadcrumbs.

Add the egg yolks and blend the mixture again, just until it comes together to form a ball of dough.

Wrap the pastry in clingfilm and chill in the refrigerator for at least 30 minutes.

Knead the pastry briefly to soften, then on a lightly floured work surface, roll out the pastry into a large circle at least 5 cm wider than the base of the tart tin.

Drape the pastry over the rolling pin, carefully lift it up and lay it over the top of the tin.

Gently press the pastry into the tin, making sure there are no air pockets, then use a sharp knife to trim off the excess pastry. Chill the tart case for 15 minutes.

Cut the nectarines or peaches in half, twist to remove the stone, then cut the fruit into slices.

Remove the pastry case from the fridge and, working from the outside, arrange the nectarine or peach slices in circles on the pastry, until all the fruit has been used.

Bake in a preheated oven at 190°C (375°F) Gas 5 for 30 minutes, then reduce the heat to 150°C (300°F) Gas 2 and continue cooking for a further 40 minutes until the fruit is tender and golden and the pastry is crisp. Dust the tart all over with icing sugar, then serve hot or cold with scoops of good-quality vanilla ice cream.

Note: This pastry is very fragile, but don't despair. Just line your tart tin as best you can, and then add extra pieces of pastry to patch up any cracks or holes.

top tip: Instead of vanilla ice cream, serve with Greek yoghurt drizzled with honey; clotted cream; crème fraîche or sweetened fromage frais.

Espresso granita

A refreshing end to a meal on a warm summer's day. Good biscotti can be purchased ready-made from Italian delis and fine food stores.

25 g sugar
3 tablespoons freshly ground coffee
biscotti, to serve
single cream, to serve (optional)

Serves 4

Put 4 small glasses or espresso cups in the freezer to chill. Put the sugar and coffee in a cafetière. Add 900 ml boiling water and let stand for 5 minutes to develop the flavour. Plunge the cafetière, pour the coffee into a heatproof jug and let cool before before chilling in the refrigerator.

When very cold, pour the coffee into a bowl and freeze for about 20 minutes, until ice crystals have formed around the edge. Crush the crystals with a fork and return to the freezer. Repeat this process about 3 times until you have an even mixture of fine ice crystals.

Cover and return to the freezer until ready to serve. Serve the granita in the serving glasses or cups with a biscotti and a drizzle of cream for anyone who prefers their coffee white.

Mini chocolate brownie squares

Everyone loves brownies – rich, sticky and chocolaty, the perfect morsel to finish off any delicious meal. They are wonderful too, served with a cup of coffee the next day.

110 g good-quality dark chocolate (70 per cent cocoa solids)
110 g butter
2 eggs, beaten
225 g caster sugar
110 g self-raising flour
50 g pecan nuts, chopped (optional)

a rectangular cake tin, 28 x 18 cm, lined with baking parchment
Makes about 54

Put the chocolate and butter in a large saucepan and melt over a low heat. Remove from the heat, add the eggs, sugar, flour and pecans, if using, and mix well. Pour into the prepared cake tin, smooth over the surface and bake in a preheated oven at 180°C (350°F) Gas 4 for 30 minutes.

Remove from the oven and let cool in the tin. When cool, lift the slab of brownies out of the tin using the baking paper, then cut into small squares.

top tip: There are more brownies in this recipe than you will need for one lunch party but they will keep for several days in an airtight container, providing you can control your intake. For a truly wicked but sensational quick pudding, take a tub of good vanilla ice cream, a punnet of raspberries and half the brownies. Let the ice cream soften a little, then spoon it into a mixing bowl. Add the raspberries and chopped brownies, mix gently, then return to the freezer for 20 minutes before serving. Yum!

Eating in the garden makes the most of heady floral fragrances and warm summer light. Shake out that crisp, linen tablecloth and wrap the cutlery in napkins. Use nature's Eden to decorate your table: gather small bunches of seasonal herbs and flowers and loosely tie them with a piece of bear grass. Lay out plump bunches of grapes and fill beautiful old plates with sugared almonds to serve with tea and coffee. It is these little touches that will make your lunch party so special and individual.

summer salads

When the markets and shops are overflowing with fresh summer produce, there is no meal quite as beautiful to look at, or as deliciously tasty, as a salad. Glossed with a mouthwatering dressing (even if it's only a little fine oil and lemon), the crisp textures, vibrant colours and wonderfully juicy flavours are ample temptation to make a healthy salad every day – so go on! Here are some ideas to get you started.

Summer beans and couscous salad

A great dish on its own, this also makes a lovely accompaniment to Rosemary and Lemon Roasted Chicken (page 58).

200 g couscous
100 g broad beans, shelled and peeled
100 g peas, shelled
100 g sugarsnap peas, trimmed
100 g runner beans, chopped
grated zest and juice of 2 lemons
5 tablespoons olive oil
2 teaspoons Spanish sweet paprika
1 garlic clove, crushed and chopped
sea salt
Serves 4

Put the couscous in a bowl, cover with boiling water, mix well, cover and let stand for 10 minutes until swollen.

Bring a large saucepan of water to the boil, then add the broad beans and cook for 5 minutes. Add the sugarsnap peas and runner beans and cook for a further 3 minutes. Drain and refresh under cold running water until the vegetables are cold (otherwise they will lose their bright fresh colour).

Drain the couscous. Transfer to a large bowl and add the beans and peas, lemon zest and juice, olive oil, paprika, garlic and salt. Mix well, then serve.

Asparagus and roasted peppers

You can make this salad on a grill pan or barbecue, or by roasting the vegetables in the oven. Take your pick – I prefer using a grill pan.

3 red peppers
2 red onions
400 g asparagus, trimmed
5 tablespoons olive oil
2 tablespoons balsamic vinegar
sea salt and freshly ground black pepper
50 g Parmesan cheese, cut into shavings, to serve (optional)
Serves 4

Cut the pepper flesh away from the core in flat pieces to make cooking easier. Put the pepper skin-side down on a preheated grill pan and cook until the skin is blistered and turning black.

Transfer the peppers to a small bowl and cover – they will continue cooking and be easier to peel. When cool, peel the skins away from the silky flesh.

Cut the onions into wedges leaving the root end intact to hold them together. Add to the grill pan and cook for 4 minutes on each side. Add the asparagus and cook for 3-4 minutes or until just soft.

Put the peppers in a bowl with the onions, asparagus, olive oil, vinegar, salt and pepper. Toss to coat, then serve with shavings of Parmesan, if using.

Mozzarella cheese with fennel and new potatoes

Mozzarella made with buffalo milk (often called *mozzarella di bufala*) has a much creamier, softer texture than mozzarella made from cow's milk. Although buffalo mozzarella is more expensive, I always use it in preference to the cow's milk variety.

200 g new potatoes
1 head of fennel
175 g mozzarella cheese
125 ml olive oil
4 tablespoons balsamic vinegar
sea salt and freshly ground black pepper

Serves 4

Cook the potatoes in a large saucepan of boiling water until just tender, about 12-14 minutes depending on their size. Drain and let cool. When the potatoes are cold, cut them in half and set aside until needed.

Trim the fennel, then cut into halves or quarters. Cut out and discard the hard central core. Using a sharp knife or a mandoline, slice the fennel very finely and set aside.

Slice the mozzarella into thin rounds.

Arrange the potatoes, fennel and mozzarella in stacks on 4 serving plates, seasoning generously between each layer with salt and pepper.

Drizzle the salads with the olive oil and sprinkle with balsamic vinegar just before serving.

Panzanella

When I find some particularly delicious bread, I always buy too much. This Tuscan salad, better made with day-old bread, is the perfect way to use up the leftovers.

4 slices country bread, cubed
4 ripe tomatoes, cut into wedges
15 cm cucumber, peeled and cut into chunks
1 red onion, sliced
a bunch of flat leaf parsley, coarsely chopped
100 g olives, pitted
50 g capers
4 tablespoons olive oil
1½ tablespoons wine vinegar
juice of ½ lemon
1 teaspoon caster sugar
sea salt and freshly ground black pepper

Serves 4

Put the bread cubes in a large bowl with the tomato, cucumber, onion and chopped parsley.

Add the olives, capers, olive oil, vinegar, lemon juice, sugar, salt and pepper, then mix well.

Leave the salad to stand for 1 hour before serving so that the bread soaks up the juices and all the flavours mingle.

top tip: This salad is highly flexible, so use whatever you have to hand – sourdough bread, a little garlic, a bunch of basil. Serve with grilled meat or fish for a hearty meal.

Summer vine tomato salad

Tomatoes vary so much. Sometimes they look fantastic but the flavour is a letdown, so it really is a case of tasting before you buy. This is not always possible, but my greengrocer lets me taste first because he knows that if I'm not happy, I will complain.

200 g sweetest vine tomatoes
15 cm cucumber
75 g pitted black olives
8 anchovy fillets
a large bunch of purple or green basil
200 g mozzarella cheese, sliced
5 tablespoons olive oil
2 tablespoons balsamic vinegar
sea salt and freshly ground black pepper

a baking sheet, lightly oiled
Serves 4

Put the tomatoes on the baking sheet and cook in a preheated oven at 130°C (250°F) Gas 1 for 1 hour. Transfer to a large salad bowl.

Peel the cucumber, cut in half lengthways and, using a teaspoon, remove all the seeds. Cut each cucumber half into 1 cm slices. Add them to the tomatoes with the olives and mix gently.

Cut the anchovy fillets into thin strips and add them to the salad bowl.

Tear the leaves from the bunch of basil and add to the bowl with the mozzarella, olive oil, vinegar, salt and pepper. Toss well and serve.

winter salads

In cold weather the marriage of salad ingredients and warm vegetables is truly scrumptious. I love the way that the warmth of the cooked food makes the salad leaves soften, adding to the succulent mixture of piquant flavours.

Warm Mediterranean Puy lentil salad

Really, this is a salad for all seasons. It works wonderfully served warm or cold and is bound to become a regular feature on your table.

100 g cherry tomatoes
300 g Puy lentils or other brown lentils
peeled rind and juice of 1 lemon
1 fresh bay leaf
2 garlic cloves, chopped
2 red onions, diced
75 g pitted garlic olives
a bunch of flat leaf parsley, coarsely chopped
4 tablespoons extra virgin olive oil
sea salt and freshly ground black pepper
100 g Parmesan or mozzarella cheese, to serve

a baking sheet, lightly oiled
Serves 4

Put the cherry tomatoes on the baking sheet and cook in a preheated oven at 130°C (250°F) Gas 1 for 40 minutes.

Put the lentils in a saucepan. Add the lemon rind and juice, bay leaf, garlic and enough water to cover. Stir, bring to the boil, then simmer for 40 minutes or until the lentils are soft.

Drain the lentils thoroughly and transfer to a large bowl. Add the tomatoes, red onion, olives, parsley, olive oil, salt and pepper, Toss gently, then serve topped with slices of Parmesan or mozzarella.

top tip: This is not only a great salad but, with various additions, can also be served as a whole meal in endless ways. Try adding bacon or ham when cooking the lentils, or some spicy sausage just before you mix everything together.

Potato and watercress with mustard seeds

For a really stylish salad, I like to use blue or purple potatoes. They have a good waxy texture that I love. If they are unavailable, use another salad-type potato – any one of your favourites will do.

400 g small potatoes, unpeeled
2 teaspoons mustard seeds
4 tablespoons olive oil
1 tablespoon white wine vinegar
200 g watercress, ends trimmed
sea salt and freshly ground pepper
Serves 4

Put the potatoes in a saucepan, cover with water, bring to the boil, then simmer for 12–14 minutes until done. Drain, then cut the potatoes into slices.

Crush the mustard seeds with a mortar and pestle, then mix in the olive oil, vinegar, salt and pepper. Pour the dressing over the potatoes and mix gently. Add the watercress, toss lightly, then serve.

Chicken liver salad

This salad makes a wonderful starter or supper dish. Be careful not to overcook the chicken livers, or they will become dry and tough, instead of perfectly cooked, juicy and soft. Chicken livers are available in butcher's shops and large supermarkets, fresh or frozen.

4 slices toasted or fried bread
200 g mixed lettuce leaves
200 g chicken livers
50 g butter
2 tablespoons olive oil
100 ml red wine
sea salt and freshly ground freshly ground black pepper

Serves 4

Put the toast on 4 small salad plates and top with the lettuce leaves.

Trim the chicken livers, removing any tubes and any dark or slightly green patches. Cut the livers into equal pieces.

Melt the butter and olive oil in a large saucepan. When really hot, add the chicken livers and cook for 2 minutes on one side, then turn them over and cook for 2 minutes more.

Add salt and pepper, then carefully remove the livers from the saucepan, using a slotted spoon, and divide them between the plates, laying them on top of the lettuce leaves.

Add the wine to the pan juices and bring to the boil, stirring. Boil hard for 1 minute, then pour the hot dressing over the livers and serve.

Roasted butternut, tomato and Parma ham salad

Butternut is the best-tasting squash on the planet, especially when roasted. I don't remove the seeds as they are edible and taste good.

1 kg butternut squash, unpeeled and cut into wedges

4 tablespoons olive oil

6 plum tomatoes, halved

12 slices Parma ham

2 bunches of rocket

sea salt and freshly ground black pepper

2-3 tablespoons pumpkin oil, to serve (optional)

a baking sheet, lightly oiled
Serves 4

Put the butternut on the baking sheet, drizzle with the olive oil and cook in a preheated oven at 180°C (350°F) Gas 4 for 35 minutes or until soft and browned at the edges. Add the tomatoes to the baking sheet for the last 15 minutes of cooking.

When cooked, remove the roasted butternut and tomatoes from the oven and divide them between 4 serving plates.

Lay the slices of Parma ham out on the same baking sheet and cook under a preheated grill for 4 minutes on each side, or until the ham is crisp and starting to brown.

Divide the rocket between the plates, putting it on top of the roasted pumpkin and tomatoes. Add the crispy Parma ham. Season with salt and pepper, drizzle the salad with a little pumpkin oil, if using, then serve.

winter lunch

Recipes here can be served at any time, mid-week or weekend, but the emphasis is on gathering the family around the table for an informal but delicious meal. There are some treats in this section that take a little time to prepare, but most of the dishes are easy one-pot recipes.

menu

Feta, onion and cucumber
salad

Vegetable couscous

Lemon tart

Chilean Merlot

Feta, onion and cucumber salad

Warm flatbread is a lovely accompaniment to this incredibly easy salad.

200 g feta cheese
6 spring onions, sliced
18 cm cucumber
a bunch of dill, coarsely chopped
2 tablespoons olive oil
1 tablespoon wine vinegar
sea salt and freshly ground black pepper

Serves 4

Crumble the feta into a salad bowl, then add the sliced spring onions.

Peel the cucumber, halve lengthways and scoop out the seeds with a teaspoon. Slice the halves into 1 cm pieces and add to the bowl.

Add the chopped dill, olive oil, vinegar, salt and pepper. Toss the salad gently and serve.

Vegetable couscous

I think this is especially good for a large gathering of people, young and old. Don't be put off by the long list of ingredients – once in the pot, it looks after itself.

2 tablespoons olive oil
2 onions, cut into wedges
2 shallots, peeled
3 garlic cloves, crushed and chopped
1 fresh red chilli, diced
1 teaspoon paprika
½ teaspoon ground cinnamon
½ teaspoon coriander seeds, crushed
½ teaspoon cumin seeds, crushed
4 cardamom pods, crushed
a large pinch of saffron strands
3 carrots, cut into 2.5 cm chunks
2 parsnips, cut into 2.5 cm chunks
½ butternut squash, cut into 2.5 cm chunks
2 courgettes, thickly sliced
1 can peeled cherry tomatoes or whole
  plum tomatoes, 400 g
600 ml vegetable stock

400 g canned chickpeas, rinsed and drained
75 g sultanas
sea salt and freshly ground black pepper
a bunch of coriander, chopped, to serve

Pine nut couscous
500 g couscous
75 g pine nuts
50 g butter, melted

Serves 4

Heat the olive oil in a large saucepan. Add the onions, shallots, garlic and chilli and cook for 2 minutes. Add the paprika, cinnamon, coriander and cumin seeds, cardamom and saffron and cook for a further 3 minutes.

Add the carrots, parsnips, butternut squash and courgettes. Cook for 5 minutes, stirring well to coat the vegetables with the spices.

Add the canned tomatoes, vegetable stock, chickpeas, sultanas, salt and pepper. Make sure all the vegetables are covered with liquid – if not, add extra stock or water as necessary. Bring to the boil and simmer for 20 minutes.

Pour the couscous into a saucepan and add enough boiling water to cover it by 2.5 cm. Bring to the boil and simmer the couscous for 3 minutes, stirring frequently. Drain well.

Put the pine nuts in a dry frying pan and cook over a medium heat, stirring constantly, until browned. Add to the drained couscous.

Pour the melted butter over the couscous and season with salt and pepper. Fluff up the grains with a fork and transfer to a large serving bowl.

Top the couscous with the cooked vegetable mixture and top with a generous quantity of chopped fresh coriander. Serve hot.

top tip: Ready-ground spices lose their flavour quickly, so it is better to buy whole seeds and crush them as needed. A mortar and pestle makes this quick and easy to do.

Lemon tart

Just about everyone loves this easy classic.

Pastry
125 g plain flour
55 g butter
25 g caster sugar
1-2 egg yolks

Lemon filling
2 eggs
175 ml double cream
50 g caster sugar
grated zest and juice of 2 lemons
25 g icing sugar, for dusting

**a loose-based flan tin, 20 cm diameter, greased
baking parchment and baking beans**

Serves 4

To make the pastry, put the flour, butter and sugar in a food processor and pulse until the mixture looks like breadcrumbs. Alternatively, put in a mixing bowl and rub with your fingertips.

Add the egg yolk and mix to a dough. Wrap it in clingfilm and chill for 30 minutes.

Roll out the pastry and line the flan tin. Gently prick the base all over with a fork, then line the pastry case with baking parchment and fill with baking beans.

Cook in a preheated oven at 200°C (400°F) Gas 6 for 20 minutes. Check after 12 minutes and reduce the heat if beginning to colour.

Remove the pastry case from the oven, remove the baking parchment and beans, and reduce the oven temperature to 170°C (325°F) Gas 3.

To make the filling, whisk the eggs in a large bowl, then mix in the cream, sugar, lemon zest and juice. Pour into the pastry case and cook for 45-50 minutes or until the lemon filling has set.

Remove from the oven and dust evenly with icing sugar. Put the tart under a very hot grill and cook until all the icing sugar has caramelized. Let cool, then serve.

Saturday family lunch

Saturdays are often rushed affairs. It is a day that seems to be dedicated to catching up on shopping, washing, cleaning, a visit to the gym or maybe recovering from that big Friday night. But please do make an effort to eat a good lunch. I have devised a meal that's simple to cook but great to eat, just for your family and friends.

menu

Garlic bread

Ratatouille

Upside-down pear cake

Loire red, such as Chinon

Garlic bread

Garlic bread is fantastic and children love it. Baguette is traditional but any bread works. Try farmhouse white, cottage loaf, ciabatta, Danish split, wholemeal, mixed grain or individual rolls and cut them accordingly.

1 loaf of bread
3 garlic cloves
100 g butter, softened
a bunch of flat leaf parsley, chopped
sea salt and freshly ground black pepper

a baking sheet
Serves 4

Cut the bread into slices without cutting the crust all the way through, or cut it in half lengthways.

Crush the whole cloves of garlic with the heel of a large knife, then peel, chop and mash to a purée with a teaspoon of salt.

Mix the garlic purée, butter, parsley, salt and pepper in a bowl, then spread generously onto the cut surfaces of the bread.

Wrap the bread in foil, put on a baking sheet and cook in a preheated oven at 180°C (350°F) Gas 4 for 20 minutes. Serve hot with ratatouille.

Variation: For quick-style garlic bread, slice the loaf and toast it on one side. Spread the other side with garlic butter, then grill.

Ratatouille

All the vegetables for ratatouille must be fresh and full of flavour in order to show off this famous French dish at its best.

3 tablespoons olive oil, plus extra to serve
2 onions, chopped
2 garlic cloves, crushed and chopped
2 red peppers, deseeded and cut into chunks
2 aubergines, cut into chunks
3 courgettes, thickly sliced
2 cans peeled plum tomatoes or
    passata, 400 g each
1/2 teaspoon dried oregano
1/2 teaspoon dried marjoram
a bunch of flat leaf parsley or basil, chopped
sea salt and freshly ground black pepper
Serves 4

Heat the olive oil in a large saucepan. Add the chopped onion and garlic and cook, stirring, for 3 minutes without browning.

Add the peppers, aubergines and courgettes to the pan and cook for 5 minutes, stirring frequently.

Add the canned tomatoes or passata, dried oregano and marjoram. Season generously with salt and pepper and stir thoroughly.

Bring the mixture to the boil, then reduce the heat under the pan and simmer for 25 minutes, stirring occasionally.

Transfer the ratatouille to a large serving bowl. Sprinkle with the chopped parsley or basil, then drizzle with some extra olive oil and serve.

top tip: Try making ratatouille the day before you plan to serve it. The flavour of the dish really seems to improve overnight and benefit from being cooled and reheated.

Upside-down pear cake

Very easy to make, this cake is a great pudding for children who want to lend a hand in the kitchen. Many types of fruit can be used in place of pears – try apples, bananas, peaches, pineapple and plums.

3 pears, peeled, halved and cored
175 g butter
175 g caster sugar
3 eggs
175 g self-raising flour, sifted
3 tablespoons milk
1 tablespoon icing sugar

a 20 cm shallow pudding dish or cake tin, greased and lined with baking parchment
Serves 4

Arrange the pear halves evenly over the bottom of the prepared pudding dish or tin and set aside.

Using an electric beater or a wooden spoon, cream the butter and sugar together in a large bowl until the mixture is light and fluffy.

Beat in the eggs, adding them one at a time and mixing well after each addition.

Add the flour to the bowl, gently fold it into the mixture, then stir in the milk.

Spoon the cake mixture evenly over the pears and smooth the surface.

Cook in a preheated oven at 180°C (350°F) Gas 4 for 45 minutes, until the surface is firm when gently touched and the cake has slightly come away from the sides of the dish.

Remove from the oven, let cool for 5 minutes, then turn out onto a serving plate. Peel away the baking parchment, dust the top of the cake evenly with icing sugar and serve immediately.

classic Sunday roast

We all love the thought of a great family Sunday roast, particularly in winter. There is nothing better than to invite people round for a traditional, slow-paced meal, the kind of dinner that our parents and grandparents do so well. I love eating from a big table in the kitchen, so the cook never misses out on the conversation and, more to the point, everyone can help. Choose whichever roast meat your family loves best – the roasting chart below is a ready-reckoner for whatever you plan to cook.

Roasting timetable

Most joints of meat or birds benefit from being put into a hot oven at 200°C (400°F) Gas 6 for the first 20 minutes to seal in the juices and keep the meat succulent, then cooked at a lower temperature 180°C (350°F) Gas 4.

Lamb

rare: 20 minutes per 500 g, plus 20 minutes

medium: 25 minutes per 500 g, plus 25 minutes

well done: 30 minutes per 500 g, plus 30 minutes

Beef

rare: 20 minutes per 500 g, plus 20 minutes

medium: 25 minutes per 500 g, plus 25 minutes

well done: 30 minutes per 500 g, plus 30 minutes

Pork

medium: 25 minutes per 500 g, plus 25 minutes

well done: 30 minutes per 500 g, plus 30 minutes

Chicken

20 minutes per 500 g, plus 20 minutes

Turkey

25 minutes per 500 g, plus 25 minutes

Venison

as for beef

Pheasant

as for chicken

Roast pork with sage and apple

There are many good cuts of pork for roasting, but my favourite is a boned and rolled loin with the skin still attached to provide that all-important crackling. Ask the butcher to score the skin thoroughly for you before rolling and tying – this helps release the fat during cooking and makes the crackling crisp and dry. This recipe gives enough for four people plus some cold meat for the next day.

1.5 kg loin of pork, boned and rolled
1 kg cooking apples, peeled and cored
50 g butter
50 ml dry cider
leaves from a bunch of sage, chopped
1 tablespoon plain flour
500 ml vegetable stock or vegetable cooking liquid
sea salt

a heavy-based roasting tin with roasting rack
Serves 4

Just before cooking, sprinkle sea salt all over the pork skin and rub in well. Place on the roasting rack.

Roast in a preheated oven at 200°C (400°F) Gas 6 for 20 minutes, then reduce the heat to 180°C (350°F) Gas 4 and cook for a further 1 hour.

Put the apples in a saucepan with the butter and cider. Cover with a lid and bring to the boil. Simmer the apples for 5 minutes, then add the chopped sage and remove the pan from the heat. Cover and set aside until needed.

When the pork is cooked, remove it from the roasting tin to a serving platter and set aside in a warm place to rest.

Using a metal spoon, skim off any excess fat from the roasting tin. Put the tin over a medium heat on top of the stove. Add the flour and use a large spoon to vigorously stir it into the meat cooking juices,

Slowly add the vegetable stock (or the same quantity of any cooking liquid from vegetables boiled for lunch), and blend with a small whisk to give a smooth sauce.

Bring to the boil and simmer for 4 minutes. Season the gravy to taste then pour into a gravy boat and serve with the roast pork and sage-flavoured apples.

menu 1

Roast pork with sage and apple

Creamy mustard mash

Braised red cabbage

Chocolate pudding cake with raspberries

Australian Semillon

menu 2

Leg of lamb with rosemary and garlic

Roasted vegetables

Minted beans and peas

Lemon meringue pie

Rhône reds

Leg of lamb with rosemary and garlic

I like my lamb pink in the middle but if you don't, adjust the cooking times according to the chart on page 79. Each piece of meat is different in weight, so do use a calculator to work out the exact roasting time.

1 leg of lamb, about 1.5 kg
5 garlic cloves, sliced
5 sprigs of rosemary, broken into small sprigs
2 tablespoons honey
2 tablespoons Dijon mustard
1 tablespoon plain flour
125 ml red wine
3 tablespoons redcurrant jelly
sea salt and freshly ground black pepper

a heavy-based roasting tin with roasting rack
Serves 4

Make incisions all over the lamb with a small, sharp knife. Insert a slice of garlic and a sprig of rosemary into each slit. Put the lamb on the rack in the roasting tin and cook in a preheated oven at 200°C (400°F) Gas 6 for 20 minutes. Lower the heat to 180°C (350°F) Gas 4 for 1 hour for rare meat.

Mix the honey and mustard together in a small jug. When the lamb has been roasting for 50 minutes, remove it from the oven and drizzle with the honey mixture. Return to the oven and roast for a further 10 minutes.

Remove the lamb from the oven, transfer to a carving board, cover with foil and set aside for 10 minutes to let the meat relax.

Put the tin over a medium heat on top of the stove, sprinkle in the flour and mix to a smooth paste. Stir in the wine, redcurrant jelly and 125 ml water. Season, bring to the boil, simmer for 3 minutes, then strain into a small jug. Carve the lamb and serve with the gravy.

With our fast pace of modern life, family roasts are all too infrequently done, which is sad as we all love them. I remember Sunday roasts as a child with great warmth and affection. We would gather round the dinner table and Dad would carve the meat.

Everyone was at home – the kitchen gathering pace with pans simmering, pastry being made, drinks being poured, vegetables peeled, herbs chopped and merry chatter and laughter. It's such a great and easy meal and all the family can be involved in preparation, children laying the table, gathering fruits or vegetables from the garden, helping in the kitchen, Mum making stuffings and sauces and always Dad pouring the drinks, choosing the wine and, for some reason, he always washed the dishes.

It's that special meal when everyone can sit around the table and share good stories from the past week and talk about exciting forthcoming projects.

Children usually love eating a roast as there are so many elements to it – delicious roasted meat, vegetables in abundance and prepared in different ways, sauces and gravy.

Then there is always the thrill and anticipation of the pudding – perhaps a pie served with lashings of cream, custard, or ice cream. Finally, for the adults, a small cup of coffee finishes off a fantastic and successful meal.

Next time you plan a Sunday roast pull out all the stops – create a happy feast and bring back good, strong, family traditions to your house. Just smell the food and listen to the laughter.

Roasted vegetables

All root vegetables are delicious roasted, but if there is something that you don't particularly like in this recipe, just remove it and replace with a family favourite.

The peeling of vegetables is a personal choice. Nutritionally, it's much better not to as many vitamins are stored just below the skin. Not peeling vegetables also saves time. However, unless your carrots are organically grown, it is essential to peel them.

3 tablespoons olive oil
4 medium potatoes, cut into chunks
4 small onions, halved with roots left intact
4 beetroot, halved
4 carrots, cut into chunks
4 parsnips, cut into chunks
sea salt and freshly ground black pepper

a roasting tin
Serves 4

Pour the oil into the roasting tin and put in a preheated oven at 200°C (400°F) Gas 6 to heat.

If the vegetables are wet, pat them dry with kitchen paper.

Remove the tin of hot oil from the oven and add the potatoes, onions and beetroot. Shake the tin until all the vegetables are coated with oil, then return to the oven and cook for 20 minutes.

Add the carrots and parsnips to the roasting tin and move all the vegetables around to ensure even cooking and colouring. Return to the oven to cook for a further 30 minutes.

Sprinkle with sea salt and freshly ground pepper and serve with the lamb.

Minted beans and peas

Mint sauce is a traditional accompaniment to roast lamb, but I haven't included it in this menu because the rosemary will have already flavoured the meat. Instead I am using mint with its other natural companion, peas, and including some delicious beans.

75 g sugarsnap peas
75 g shelled broad beans
75 g runner beans, sliced
75 g shelled fresh peas
leaves from a bunch of mint, chopped
1½ tablespoons butter
sea salt and freshly ground black pepper
Serves 4

Bring a large saucepan of water to the boil. Add the peas and beans all at once, return to the boil and simmer for 3 minutes.

Drain, then return the peas and beans to the pan. Add the mint, butter, salt and pepper. Toss well and serve immediately.

Creamy mustard mash

Mashed potato with mustard is, for me, true comfort food on an autumn or winter day. For a change, try adding a mixture of grated cheese, chopped herbs and chopped spring onions or fried onions. To give the mash a spicy kick, stir in some finely chopped red chillies and a drizzle of chilli oil.

750 g potatoes, cut into large cubes
150 ml milk
3 tablespoons olive oil
50 g butter
1 tablespoon powdered English mustard
sea salt and freshly ground black pepper
Serves 4

Put the potatoes in a saucepan of water, bring to the boil, then lower the heat and simmer for 20 minutes or until tender.

Drain the cooked potatoes thoroughly, then return them to the pan and set it over a low heat. Shake the pan and let the potatoes steam dry.

Put the milk, olive oil and butter in a separate saucepan and warm gently.

Mash the potatoes well, being sure to crush out all the lumps. Alternatively, press the potatoes through a potato ricer.

Add the warm milk mixture, mustard, salt and pepper to the mashed potatoes. Using a wooden spoon, beat well until smooth and well blended. Taste and adjust the seasoning as necessary.

top tip: Never try to mash potatoes in a food processor or blender, it will make them gluey. If cooking the mash a little in advance of serving, cover the potatoes with some buttered greaseproof paper and keep warm.

Braised red cabbage

This deliciously fruity winter vegetable dish can be made in advance and reheated – it actually improves with time and a second cooking. It is good served with most roast meats and is a favourite component of the Scandinavian Christmas Eve dinner of roast pork, goose or duck.

25 g butter
1 onion, chopped
750 g red cabbage, cored and finely sliced
2 cooking apples, cored, peeled and chopped
125 g sultanas
2 tablespoons brown sugar
2 tablespoons white wine vinegar
sea salt and freshly ground black pepper
Serves 4

Melt the butter in a large saucepan. Add the onion and cook over a low heat until softened.

Add the cabbage, apples, sultanas, 175 ml water, sugar and vinegar. Season and mix well.

Cover with a lid, bring to the boil, then reduce the heat and simmer for about 1 hour until tender. Check the cabbage occasionally, adding more water if needed.

Remove the lid and cook uncovered for a further 15 minutes. Adjust the seasoning, then serve hot.

top tip: For a festive flavour, add a couple of whole cloves, a bay leaf, a strip of orange peel and some red wine at the same time as the cabbage.

Good old-fashioned puddings never really go out of fashion and are tops when it comes to cosy Sunday lunches with the family. Take a tip from grandma and keep portions on the generous side of large.

Chocolate pudding cake with raspberries

'Simple, pure indulgence' could be another name for this delicious and versatile pud. If you prefer, it can be made the day before and stored in the fridge, then served at room temperature. Consider also putting it on the menu for dinner parties or afternoon tea.

250 g good-quality dark chocolate (70 per cent cocoa solids)
200 g butter
1 teaspoon instant coffee, dissolved in 1 tablespoon hot water
5 eggs
100 g caster sugar
75 g plain flour
150 g raspberries
icing sugar or cocoa powder, for dusting
175 ml single cream, to serve

a springform cake tin, 23 cm diameter, greased and lined with baking
   parchment
Serves 4–6

Put the chocolate, butter and instant coffee mixture in a saucepan over a very low heat and stir until smooth. Remove from the heat and set aside.

Crack the eggs into a mixing bowl, add the sugar and whisk with an electric beater until light and fluffy, about 5 minutes.

Add the flour and chocolate mixture to the fluffy eggs and use a large metal spoon to fold them together until smooth.

Pour the batter into the prepared cake tin, sprinkle with the raspberries and bake in a preheated oven at 170°C (325°F) Gas 3 for 40 minutes or until the cake is firm to the touch and has come away from the sides of the tin.

Dust with icing sugar or cocoa and serve with cream.

Lemon meringue pie

This lovely traditional pudding may seem complicated, but believe me it's worth it – the combination is heavenly and once you've made it, I think you'll cook it all the time. Don't ever skimp on the meringue – it has to be piled high to have the wow-factor. Try replacing the lemon with lime or orange and, for special occasions, try making this recipe into small individual tarts.

250 g plain flour, plus extra for dusting
125 g butter, cut into small pieces
30 g caster sugar
2 egg yolks

Lemon filling
grated zest and juice of 3 lemons
125 g caster sugar
50 g butter
40 g cornflour
3 egg yolks

Meringue
3 egg whites
175 g caster sugar

a loose-based flan tin, 20 cm diameter,
baking parchment and baking beans or uncooked rice
Serves 4–6

To make the pastry, sift the flour into a bowl, then rub in the butter with your fingertips until it looks like fine breadcrumbs. Stir in the sugar.

Add the egg yolks and, using a round-bladed knife, cut through the mixture until the pastry starts to clump together. Knead briefly to ensure even mixing, then cover with clingfilm and chill for 10 minutes.

Lightly dust a work surface with flour, then roll out the pastry and use it to line the flan tin. Cover and chill for 30 minutes.

Gently prick the base of the pastry case with a fork, then line with baking parchment and fill with baking beans or uncooked rice. Cook in a preheated oven at 190°C (375°F) Gas 5 for 15 minutes.

Remove the pastry case from the oven and reduce the heat to 170°C (325°F) Gas 3. Lift the baking parchment and beans or rice out of the pastry case and return the case to the oven for a further 5–10 minutes to dry out a little.

Meanwhile, to make the filling, put the lemon zest and juice into a small saucepan with the sugar, butter and cornflour. Stir, then gently heat to simmering point. When the mixture is thick, remove it from the heat and let cool for 5 minutes.

Beat the egg yolks into the filling and spoon into the cooked pastry case.

To make the meringue, whisk the egg whites with an electric beater until stiff and standing in peaks. Add half the sugar and whisk well, then quickly whisk in the remaining sugar.

Pile the meringue on top of the lemon filling. Spread it evenly over the top and seal the meringue to the edge of the pastry case.

Cook in a preheated oven at 170°C (325°F) Gas 3 for 15 minutes until the meringue is lightly golden. Serve hot (great) or cold (irresistible).

working lunch

In most people's working lives, every minute counts, but health must also be a priority. Remember that what we eat can make us feel good and work more efficiently. Try making your own lunch to take to work. When using these recipes, everyone will watch you enviously as you calmly sit at your desk and unwrap each day's delight.

Chill the soup overnight until very cold. Transfer to a thermos flask and chill until ready to serve.

Cheesy stuffed croissants

A great portable snack, best made with your favourite cheese – I like Gruyère or brie. This is the classic recipe, but you can use sliced tomatoes or lightly cooked sliced mushrooms instead of the ham.

4 croissants
2 teaspoons Dijon mustard
4 slices cheese
4 thick slices Black Forest smoked ham
freshly ground black pepper

a baking sheet
Serves 4

Cut the croissants in half lengthways and open out. Spread each croissant with ½ teaspoon Dijon mustard, then add the cheese, ham and pepper.

Transfer to a baking sheet and cook in a preheated oven at 180°C (350°F) Gas 4 for 10 minutes. Serve hot or cold.

Gazpacho soup

This soup tastes wonderful but is also very nutritious thanks to all the vitamin-rich raw ingredients. On a less healthy note, it also makes a terrific base for a totally delicious Bloody Mary!

1 onion, chopped
2 slices white bread, crusts removed
2 red peppers, deseeded and diced
15 cm cucumber, peeled
1 garlic clove, crushed and chopped
4 celery stalks, diced
600 ml tomato passata

3 tablespoons olive oil
½ tablespoon white wine vinegar
a dash of Tabasco sauce
sea salt and freshly ground black pepper
Serves 4

Put the onion in a blender and whizz to a fine dice. Tear or dice the bread and add to the blender with the peppers, cucumber, garlic and celery. Whizz until finely chopped.

Add the passata, 300 ml water, olive oil, vinegar, Tabasco, salt and pepper. Blend for 3 minutes, then pour into chilled bowls and serve.

Salad box

Very simple and flexible, this lunch box can include whatever things are in your fridge.

1 aubergine, sliced lengthways
4 courgettes, sliced lengthways
1 can butter beans, 400 g, rinsed and drained
300 g cooked penne pasta
4 tomatoes, sliced
4 hard-boiled eggs, shelled and halved
a bunch of flat leaf parsley, chopped
4 tablespoons caperberries, or 4 teaspoons
  capers, rinsed and drained
4 tablespoons olive oil
2 tablespoons balsamic vinegar
100 g Parmesan cheese, shaved with a peeler
1 lemon, quartered lengthways
sea salt and freshly ground black pepper

Serves 4

Cook the aubergines and courgettes on a stove-top grill pan on medium heat for 5 minutes each side.

Divide the butter beans and cooked pasta between 4 lunch boxes. Add the aubergines, courgettes, tomatoes, boiled eggs, parsley and caperberries or capers.

Sprinkle the salads with the olive oil and balsamic vinegar. Season with salt and pepper and top with shavings of Parmesan.

Add a wedge of lemon to each box, put on the lids and chill overnight. Take to work and eat at room temperature.

Chicken salad wrap

4 soft flour tortillas, preferably wholemeal
4 tablespoons mayonnaise
2 teaspoons wholegrain mustard
2 cooked chicken breasts, shredded
2 carrots, grated
a wedge of white cabbage, finely sliced
2 medium tomatoes, finely sliced
sea salt and freshly ground black pepper
Serves 4

Lay each tortilla flat on a piece of greaseproof paper. Spread with the mayonnaise and mustard.

Add the shredded chicken, grated carrot, sliced cabbage, salt, pepper and tomato.

Roll up the tortillas into tight cylinders, using the greaseproof paper to help you. Twist the ends of the paper together.

Cut the cylinders in half diagonally. Wrap each portion in clingfilm and chill until ready for work.

top tip: If you want to make your own lunches, a clever trick is to keep it in mind the night before when you are cooking dinner. Any extra chicken, meats, fish, boiled eggs, potatoes, pasta, rice or roasted vegetables such as pumpkin, peppers or onions can be incorporated in a wonderful sandwich or salad.

Chicken and vegetable satay sticks with noodle salad

Satays look spectacular, so this is a perfect lunch to serve at meetings. It also caters for any vegetarians who may be in the group. Soaking the satay sticks is important – it prevents them burning under the grill.

2 chicken breasts
1 aubergine, cut into 8 chunks
8 mushrooms
2 courgettes, cut into 8 chunks
1 red or yellow pepper, cut into 8 chunks
185 ml soy sauce
3 tablespoons smooth peanut butter
2 tablespoons vegetable oil
1 onion, sliced
1 garlic clove, crushed and chopped
2.5 cm fresh ginger, peeled and sliced
100 g beanthread noodles
100 g chopped peanuts
a bunch of coriander leaves

16 wooden satay sticks, soaked in water for
    at least 30 minutes
a baking sheet, lightly oiled
Serves 4

Cut each chicken breast into 4 strips, then thread onto 8 of the soaked satay sticks.

Push the aubergine, mushrooms, courgettes and pepper alternately onto another 8 satay sticks.

Put 125 ml of the soy sauce in a bowl or jug, add the peanut butter and 4 tablespoons water. Use this mixture to baste the satay sticks.

Arrange the sticks on the oiled baking sheet and cook under a preheated grill for 12 minutes, turning occasionally until evenly browned.

Heat the oil in a wok or frying pan. Add the onion, garlic and ginger and stir-fry over a medium heat without browning.

Meanwhile, bring a large saucepan of water to the boil. Add the noodles, boil for 1 minute, then drain immediately.

Add the noodles to the wok with the peanuts, coriander and the remaining soy sauce. Stir well.

Divide the mixture between 4 lunch boxes and top with the cooked satay sticks. Let cool, then chill overnight. If you're taking this to work, store the boxes in the office fridge and remove them 20 minutes before serving.

To help fit everything into your day, have some informal meetings round a conference table laid out with a delicious but easy-to-eat lunch. That's delicious time management...

food on the move

This is a very modern way of eating. Since we all lack time, we have to utilize it cleverly, so sitting on a train or taking a walk while snacking is increasingly common. But food taken on the hoof can be a treat – take inspiration from these recipes and enjoy the freedom.

Tomato and goats' cheese tart

Oh, how I love this tart – the crumbly, flaky texture of the puff pastry, the finely sliced onions and roasted tomatoes, then melted goats' cheese binding them altogether. Puff pastry can be bought frozen or from the chiller cabinets. It even comes pre-rolled for the super-busy person. I think it's always worth having a packet in the freezer as it is very versatile and can be quickly made into savoury or sweet tarts.

375 g ready-made puff pastry
2 onions, finely sliced
200 g roasted baby tomatoes (page 69)
150 g soft, rindless goats' cheese, crumbled
2 tablespoons olive oil
1 teaspoon caster sugar
sea salt and freshly ground black pepper

a baking sheet, lightly oiled
a saucer, 15 cm diameter
Serves 4

Roll out the pastry and cut 4 circles using the saucer as a template. Transfer to the baking sheet. Prick the pastry all over with a fork.

Bake in a preheated oven at 190°C (375°F) Gas 5 for 15 minutes, then remove from the oven, but leave the oven at the same temperature.

Put the sliced onion in a bowl with the tomatoes, goats' cheese, olive oil, sugar, salt and pepper and mix well. Divide the mixture between the pastry bases, spreading it evenly over the top and pushing down gently.

Return the tarts to the oven and cook for 20 minutes, then reduce the heat to 180°C (350°F) Gas 4 and cook for a further 15–20 minutes until lightly browned. Serve hot or at room temperature.

Steak and tomato sandwich

Such a classic sandwich and really very delicious! Always use very fresh bread and for this, I think unbleached bread is best.

olive oil, for greasing
4 sirloin steaks, 100 g each
8 slices bread
butter, for spreading
4 teaspoons Dijon mustard
2 beef tomatoes, sliced
2 bunches of rocket, about 100 g
sea salt and freshly ground black pepper

Serves 4

Heat a stove-top grill pan or a non-stick frying pan with a little olive oil. When very hot, add the steaks and cook 1 minute on each side for rare steak, 2 minutes each side for medium or 3 minutes each side for well done.

Meanwhile, spread 4 slices of the bread with butter and mustard, then add the sliced tomatoes and rocket.

Top with the cooked steak and sprinkle with salt and pepper. Butter the remaining slices of bread and put them on top of the steaks. Press together, wrap in a napkin and eat as you walk out of the house.

Hoummus and salad in Turkish flatbread

If Turkish flatbread is hard to find, use pita bread instead – just toast it lightly, open up the pocket and fill with all the ingredients given here.

4 sheets very thin Turkish flatbread
175 g hoummus
¼ head iceberg lettuce
2 avocados, halved, pitted and sliced
juice of 1 lemon
2 tablespoons olive oil
sea salt and freshly ground black pepper

Serves 4

Open out the flatbreads and lay each one on a piece of greaseproof paper. Spread evenly with the hoummus.

Shred the iceberg lettuce finely and scatter it over the bread. Arrange the sliced avocado on top, then sprinkle with the lemon juice and olive oil. Season generously with salt and pepper.

With the help of the greaseproof paper, roll up the bread and filling tightly and shape with your hands into a cylinder, twisting the paper at each end.

Cut the cylinders in half, then wrap in a napkin and go. Eat the wraps within 3 hours of making for a really good, fresh taste.

Focaccia with grilled chicken

This sandwich is a meal in itself: wrap it in clingfilm and eat it on long-distance journeys. Choose buffalo milk mozzarella whenever possible – it's indisputably better than cows' milk.

2 chicken fillets, halved lengthways
1 loaf focaccia bread
1 garlic clove, halved lengthways
2 tomatoes, sliced
150 g mozzarella cheese, sliced
a large bunch of basil, leaves torn
2 tablespoons olive oil
sea salt and freshly ground black pepper

Serves 4

Cook the chicken on a preheated stove-top grill pan or under a grill for about 5–6 minutes on each side, or until cooked right through. Remove and set aside.

Cut the focaccia in half lengthways and put the bread cut-side down on the grill pan or cut-side up under the grill. Cook until lightly toasted.

Remove the bread from the heat and rub the toasted surface with the garlic clove.

Put a piece of focaccia, toasted-side up, on a board. Top with the chicken, tomatoes, cheese, basil, olive oil, salt and pepper.

Cover with a second piece of focaccia and press down. Repeat with the remaining ingredients.

Cut into portions, wrap in clingfilm or cellophane and put in bags or boxes for transport.

Ham and thyme tortilla

The Spaniards serve tortilla as a tapas snack. It is delicious cold too, so makes the ideal meal for people on the go.

3 medium potatoes
3 tablespoons olive oil
2 onions, sliced
100 g ham, chopped
5 eggs
4 tablespoons milk
leaves from 8 sprigs of thyme, coarsely chopped
75 g Gruyère cheese, grated
sea salt and freshly ground black pepper

an ovenproof frying pan
Serves 4–6

Cook the potatoes in boiling water until just tender. Drain and cool, then slice.

Heat the olive oil in a medium frying pan. Add the onions and cook over a moderate heat for 7 minutes or until soft and lightly golden. Add the ham and potatoes and mix thoroughly.

Beat the eggs in a bowl, then add the milk, chopped thyme, salt and pepper. Pour into the frying pan and mix carefully.

Sprinkle with the cheese and cook over a medium heat for 8 minutes. Reduce the heat and cook for another 10 minutes, until the egg has almost set.

Put the pan under a pre-heated grill and cook until the cheese is golden and bubbling.

Remove from the heat. Check that the tortilla is firm, then turn it upside down onto a plate. Put another plate on top and turn the tortilla over again to reveal the golden cheesy topping. Serve.

The secret of good food on the move is practical packaging. Keep a selection of sturdy boxes, greaseproof paper, cellophane bags and cloth or paper napkins ready to wrap your snack foods. Some things, such as the tortilla, travel better whole, so take it in the pan and carry a small knife with you to cut it into wedges when hungry.

snack attack

We all get the munchies, but next time, instead of reaching for that packet of crisps or bar of chocolate, make a little effort and try preparing one of these snacks. Pure, fresh and nutritious food, they will stop all rumblings in your tummy and taste good too.

Courgettes and Cheddar on toast

This simple combination tastes like heaven – just make sure that you squeeze the grated courgette well.

2 courgettes, grated
200 g mature Cheddar cheese, grated
1 shallot, finely diced
1 small egg
a dash of Worcestershire sauce
4 slices bread, toasted
sea salt and freshly ground black pepper

a baking sheet
Serves 4

Put the grated courgettes in a tea towel and twist tightly, squeezing out all the excess liquid.

Transfer to a mixing bowl and add the cheese, shallot, egg, Worcestershire sauce, salt and pepper. Stir thoroughly.

Put the toasted bread onto the baking sheet, pile the courgette mixture on top and cook under a preheated grill until golden brown. Serve hot.

Banana smoothie

To me, this is bliss in the summer and it quickly rids me of any hunger pangs.

4 large, ripe bananas
500 ml cold milk
250 ml ice
2 tablespoons honey
1 tablespoon rolled oats
1 tablespoon bran
Serves 4

Chop the bananas into a blender. Add all the remaining ingredients and whizz until smooth. Serve in large glasses and taste the goodness.

Mountain eggs

I first came across this dish in the Swiss Alps where they cook and serve it in small, individual frying pans. Whenever hunger struck us between meals, we rushed straight into a little restaurant for a pan of these eggs. Ham is traditional, but this is also very good with chorizo sausage. If you are vegetarian, replace the ham with mushrooms.

4 teaspoons olive oil
4 large cooked potatoes, sliced 2.5 cm thick
200 g smoked ham, chopped
4 eggs
4 slices Emmental cheese, 1 cm thick,
    or 100 g grated Emmental
sea salt and freshly ground black pepper
chopped flat leaf parsley, to serve (optional)

Serves 4

Heat 1 teaspoon of oil in each of 4 small frying pans. Add the potatoes and cook for 2 minutes on each side. Stir in the ham.

Crack an egg into each pan. Top with the sliced or grated cheese, sprinkle with salt and pepper and cook for 2–3 minutes until the egg is just set and the cheese is beginning to melt.

Serve sprinkled with chopped parsley, if using.

Blue cheese and tomato crostini

Here is a fantastic snack to enjoy while relaxing with a glass of wine or beer and some friends. If you do not like blue cheese, Italian mozzarella or Taleggio, or soft goats' milk varieties are good alternatives.

4 slices sourdough bread, or 8 slices baguette
1 garlic clove
2 tablespoons olive oil
100 g blue cheese
2 tomatoes, sliced
sea salt and black pepper
Serves 4

Toast the bread slices on each side. Rub them with the garlic, using it like a grater, then sprinkle each slice with ½ tablespoon olive oil.

Crumble half the blue cheese with your fingers and divide it between the 4 slices of toast.

Top with the sliced tomatoes, in a single layer, then cover with the remaining cheese. Sprinkle lightly with salt and pepper.

Cook the crostini under a hot grill, until the cheese melts and begins to brown lightly, about 4–5 minutes. Serve hot or warm.

Afternoon tea is such a pretty meal, so go with it: dig out that beautiful floral china your grandmother gave you, shake an embroidered cloth on the table and get baking. When your friends arrive at 4 pm, pour steaming cups of tea, spread scones with strawberry jam and giggle the hours away – what fun!

teatime

Sodabread

Country people work hard and the traditional way to top up their energy levels is with a substantial meal at teatime. Served with a good, flavourful Cheddar, this lovely bread provides the perfect boost.

500 g wholemeal flour
1 teaspoon bicarbonate of soda
1 teaspoon cream of tartar
a pinch of salt
25 g butter, cut into small cubes
300 ml milk

a baking sheet, lightly floured
Makes 1 loaf

Sift the flour, bicarbonate of soda, cream of tartar and salt into a large bowl. Rub the butter into the flour with your fingertips.

Make a well in the centre. Pour in the milk and mix with a round-bladed knife to form a soft dough.

Turn out the dough onto a lightly floured surface and knead until smooth, about 4 minutes. Shape the dough into a round loaf 15 cm in diameter and flatten the top slightly.

Place on the baking sheet and use a sharp knife to score a cross about 1 cm deep in the top of the dough, making quarters.

Bake in a preheated oven at 180°C (350°F) Gas 4 for 35 minutes. Remove from the oven and, protecting your hands with a tea towel, tap the bottom of the loaf with your knuckles – when cooked, it should sound hollow; if it doesn't, bake for a few minutes more.

Serve warm, topped with slices of mature Cheddar cheese or spread with butter and jam.

top tip: Sandwiches are a must at teatime. Try making them with a variety of all the great breads that are available in the stores. Good combinations include sodabread with egg or tuna, walnut bread with Cheddar and finely sliced celery, sourdough with smoked ham, focaccia with smoked salmon and pepper or ciabatta with mozzarella and basil.

Cucumber sandwiches with cream cheese

If you want to be truly traditional, remove the crusts with a serrated knife and cut

each sandwich into 3 fingers before serving. When I make them, I leave the crusts on and cut the sandwiches into 4 fingers.

20 cm cucumber
8 slices mixed grain bread
butter, for spreading
100 g cream cheese
sea salt and freshly ground black pepper
Serves 4

Peel and finely slice the cucumber.

Spread each slice of bread lightly with the butter. Take 4 slices and spread them with a layer of cream cheese. Sprinkle some salt and pepper over the top, then add a generous layer of the sliced cucumber.

Place a second slice of bread on top of each sandwich, carefully press together, then cut.

Egg and cress rolls

Summer days and teatime on a rug in the garden with egg and cress rolls – happy memories of my childhood. It makes me smile and want to start boiling eggs!

3 hard-boiled eggs, shelled and chopped
1 tablespoon mayonnaise
1 punnet mustard and cress, or a small bunch of watercress, trimmed
4 soft bread rolls
butter, for spreading
sea salt and freshly ground black pepper

Makes 4

Put the eggs and mayonnaise in a bowl, season and mix well. Cut the mustard and cress from the punnet, or trim the watercress.

Cut the bread rolls in half and spread lightly with butter. Fill with the egg mayonnaise and top with the mustard and cress. Close the rolls and serve.

Sultana scones

If friends turn up on your doorstep and catch you unprepared, scones are incredibly easy and speedy to make, and they're best eaten straight out of the oven. All you need then is butter and rich fruit jam.

500 g self-raising flour
125 g butter, cut into small pieces
100 g sultanas
300 ml milk, plus extra for glazing

a baking sheet, lightly dusted with flour
a 6-cm plain biscuit cutter
Makes 8

Sift the flour into a large mixing bowl, then rub in the butter with your fingertips until the mixture looks like fine breadcrumbs. Stir in the sultanas.

Make a well in the centre and pour in the milk. Mix with a round-bladed knife until the mixture is soft and spongy.

Turn out the dough onto a lightly floured work surface and knead it for 2–3 minutes until smooth.

Press or roll out the dough to a thickness of 2.5 cm. Using the biscuit cutter lightly dusted with flour, cut out 6–8 rounds. Brush the tops of the scones with a little milk.

Put on the baking sheet and cook in a preheated oven at 220°C (425°F) Gas 7 for 10–12 minutes. Remove from the oven and eat hot or warm.

top tip: You can make many variations on this reliable scone recipe by using other fruit instead of the sultanas. Don't restrict yourself to dried varieties — even fresh fruit such as finely chopped apple, apricots, bananas or cherries work well. Choose a jam to match for real pizzazz.

Lemon and ginger infusion

This delicious hot drink can also help to soothe a sore throat. If you want to give it a festive kick, add a dash of whisky.

zest and juice of 3 lemons
5 cm fresh ginger, peeled and sliced
a bunch of mint leaves

To serve

2.5 cm fresh ginger, peeled and finely sliced
1 lemon, finely sliced
sugar or honey (optional)

Serves 4

Put the lemon zest and juice, ginger and mint in a heatproof jug. Pour on 750 ml boiling water and let steep for about 6 minutes.

Serve hot in teacups with slices of ginger and lemon. Sweeten to taste with sugar or honey.

Iced jasmine tea

Keep this refreshing and cooling drink in the fridge to sip throughout a hot summer day.

2 teaspoons jasmine tea
ice cubes (see method)
2 peaches, pitted and sliced
1 lemon, sliced

Serves 4

Put the tea in a jug, add 750 ml boiling water and brew for 5 minutes. Strain and let cool.

Half-fill a glass serving jug with ice cubes, add the sliced peaches and lemon, then pour over the cooled tea and mix well. Serve immediately.

Strawberry tarts

I can't resist these very special tarts, and when the strawberry season is at its peak I make them often.

300 g plain flour
150 g butter
150 g caster sugar
4 egg yolks
175 g redcurrant jelly
500 g strawberries, hulled but left whole

To serve

icing sugar, for dusting
about 250 ml whipped cream

6–8 loose-based tartlet tins, 10 cm diameter, lightly greased
baking parchment and baking beans or uncooked rice

Makes 6–8

Put the flour in a large mixing bowl, then rub in the butter with your fingertips until the mixture looks like fine readcrumbs.

Using a round-bladed knife, mix in the sugar, then the egg yolks until the dough forms a ball. If the mixture is too dry, add 1 tablespoon of water.

Turn out the dough onto a lightly floured work surface. Knead quickly until the pastry is smooth, then wrap in clingfilm and chill for 20 minutes.

Put the chilled pastry on a lightly floured work surface. Roll out to about 8 mm thick, then use to line the tartlet tins.

Prick the base of each pastry case a few times with a fork, then line with baking parchment and baking beans or rice. Bake in a preheated oven at 200°C (400°F) Gas 6 for 15 minutes.

Remove the tartlet cases from the oven and lift out the paper and baking beans or rice. Return the cases to the oven for a further 10 minutes, until the pastry is set and light golden. Remove from the oven and let cool in the tins.

Melt the redcurrant jelly in a small saucepan with 2 tablespoons water. When the pastry cases are cool, brush the interiors with a little glaze and let set (this stops the fruit juices making the pastry soggy).

Arrange the strawberries in the pastry cases.

Add 1 tablespoon water to the glaze left in the saucepan and heat through. Brush or spoon the glaze over the fruit and let cool and set.

Remove the tartlets from the tins, dust lightly with icing sugar and then serve with a little whipped cream.

Lemon syrup cake

This really is the simplest yet most delicious cake ever. In our house we can't even wait for it to cool before tucking in!

250 g butter
250 g caster sugar
4 eggs
grated zest of 4 lemons
250 g self-raising flour, sifted

Lemon syrup
juice of 4 lemons
150 g caster sugar

a 1.25 kg loaf tin, 22 x 12 cm, greased
Makes 1 loaf

Cream the butter and sugar in a large mixing bowl until light and soft. Beat in the eggs one at a time. Using a metal spoon, carefully fold in the lemon zest and flour.

Place in the prepared tin and bake in a preheated oven at 200°C (400°F) Gas 6 for 35 minutes.

Insert a knife or skewer in the middle of the cake – if it comes out clean, the cake is cooked. If not, return it to the oven for another 5 minutes.

Remove the cake from the oven, let cool in the tin for 5 minutes, then turn out onto a plate.

To make the lemon syrup, put the lemon juice and sugar in a small saucepan and heat gently until the sugar has melted.

Spike the cake with a skewer and spoon the syrup over the top, allowing it to slowly sink in. Repeat until all the syrup has been used.

Celebration iced fruit cake

Although this moist cake takes quite a long time to cook – 3½ hours – to mark a family celebration, it really is worth it.

350 g raisins
350 g currants
350 g sultanas
150 g chopped mixed peel
100 g undyed glacé cherries
325 g butter, melted
300 g light brown sugar
4 eggs
300 g plain flour
2 teaspoons mixed spice
½ teaspoon ground cinnamon
a pinch of freshly grated nutmeg
3 tablespoons Madeira or sherry, plus extra
  for sprinkling (optional)

Icing
2 tablespoons apricot jam
icing sugar, for dusting
500 g ready-to-roll marzipan
500 g ready-to-roll white icing

a loose-based cake tin, 20 cm diameter, greased
  and lined with baking parchment
Makes 1 cake

Put the dried fruits, peel and glacé cherries in a large bowl and mix well. Add the melted butter, sugar, eggs, flour, mixed spice, cinnamon, nutmeg and the Madeira or sherry. Mix well.

Spoon the mixture into the prepared cake tin and bake on the middle rack of a preheated oven at 150°C (300°F) Gas 2. Cook for 3–3½ hours or until a skewer inserted in the centre of the cake comes out clean.

When cooked, let the cake cool in the tin for 25 minutes, then remove from the tin and let cool completely on a wire rack.

If you like a really boozy, moist cake, drizzle with an extra spoonful of Madeira or sherry before wrapping the cake in paper. Store in a cake tin or wrapped in clingfilm for up to 3 weeks.

A few days before the celebration, ice the cake. Melt the apricot jam with ½ tablespoon water. Put the cake on a flat serving plate and brush the top and sides of the cake with a little warm jam.

On a work surface dusted with icing sugar, roll out the marzipan to 5 mm thick. Measure the height of the cake and its circumference, then cut a rectangular strip of marzipan to fit those measurements. Wrap it around the cake, pressing the join together to seal.

Using a plate or the cake tin as a template, cut a circle of marzipan to fit the top of the cake exactly. Lay it over the cake and smooth out with your hands. Use a pin to burst any air bubbles and gently press the air out with your fingers.

Brush the marzipan surface of the cake with water. Repeat the same process you used with the marzipan using the ready-to-roll icing, making sure the surface is dusted with icing sugar to prevent sticking. Use your fingers to rub all the joins carefully together (the more you rub, the more invisible they become).

Again, prick any air holes with a pin and press out the air. Store the cake in an airtight container until needed. I like my cake pure and simple and decorated with a few buds or petals and maybe a beautiful gauze ribbon tied around the side.

top tip: To make a special but small gift for someone, make this cake and then wrap it in cellophane with a lovely bow and write a message on a tag.

Coconut jam biscuits

200 g caster sugar
200 g butter, softened
150 g desiccated coconut
2 eggs
200 g plain flour
1 jar fruit rich jam, about 340 g

a baking sheet, lined with baking parchment
Makes 12

Put the sugar and butter in a bowl and cream until light and fluffy.

Add the coconut and eggs, mix well, then sift in the flour and stir until smooth.

Using 2 teaspoons, shape the mixture into balls and put onto the prepared baking sheet, spaced about 1 cm apart – don't sit them too close to each other as the biscuits need room to spread while in the oven.

Bake in a preheated oven at 180°C (250°F) Gas 4 for 10–12 minutes until lightly golden.

Remove from the oven and let cool and set for 5 minutes on the baking sheet. Then remove to a wire rack to cool completely.

Repeat until all the biscuit mixture is used, making at least 24 biscuits.

When the biscuits are cool, spread the flat side of each one with ½ teaspoon jam and sandwich together. Store in an airtight tin and eat quickly.

top tip: To vary these biscuits, sandwich them together with other fillings. Try a different fruit jam, some lemon or other citrus curd, sweetened prune purée or decadent cream cheese frosting mixed with candied peel.

night

The more life rushes by, the more I think it is important to make a good evening meal, pour a glass of wine or shake a cocktail, lay a table or tray, and then laugh the day away with your family or friends. No matter how hectic the day has been, it's possible to prepare a good home-cooked meal in the evening. There are plenty of ideas in this chapter for one-pot and one-bowl meals to eat informally, but even the party food and romantic dinners featured here can be quickly rustled up. For special occasions, it's fun to make a little fuss and throw an extravagant party. I enjoy planning the perfect menu and setting the scene with flowers, twinkling candles and my favourite tableware. After the feast, serve rich chocolates with fresh, steaming-hot coffee in small glasses (very cosmopolitan) and chat away with your friends until the early hours — what a delightful way to end the day and start tomorrow.

weekday suppers store cupboard basics supper on a tray comfort food

one-pot meals smart drinks and finger food party time supper for friends

twilight barbecue dinner party dream dinner date late night feast

weekday suppers

This is what I call 'Formula-One cooking' – fast, furious and delivering a podium-stand winner for supper. It's so simple. From spinach salad with bacon dressing to a racy Thai noodle salad via lemon spaghetti oozing with fresh citrus flavours. If these win in your house, why not pop open the champagne and take a bow?

Spinach and bacon salad with Dijon dressing

200 g young spinach leaves, trimmed, washed and dried in a salad spinner
4 hard-boiled eggs, shelled and quartered
12 cherry tomatoes, halved
12 slices bacon, grilled, then chopped
2 avocados, halved, deseeded and chopped
wholegrain bread, to serve

Dijon dressing
juice of 1 lemon
1 tablespoon white wine vinegar
1 teaspoon Dijon mustard
4 tablespoons sunflower or vegetable oil
1 teaspoon caster sugar
sea salt and freshly ground black pepper

Serves 4

Put the spinach in a bowl. Add the quartered eggs, cherry tomatoes, bacon and avocados.

To make the dressing, mix the lemon juice, vinegar and mustard together in a bowl, then slowly whisk in the oil.

Stir the sugar, salt and pepper into the dressing. Mix well, pour over the salad and serve with chunks of wholegrain bread.

top tip: For perfect hard-boiled eggs, cook them in simmering water for about 9 minutes, then drain and run under cold water until the eggs are quite cold. To peel, gently tap them on a flat, hard surface to crack the shells all over, then peel under running water. If eggs are very fresh the shell won't come away easily from the white — so, if the peeled egg looks messy, at least you know it was really fresh.

Lemon spaghetti

This is a favourite meal in our house – it's delicious and very quick to make. If more sustenance is needed, grill some fish such as halibut or skate and serve on top.

300 g dried spaghetti
1 garlic clove, chopped
grated zest and juice of 2 lemons
4 tablespoons olive oil
125 g Parmesan cheese, freshly grated
a bunch of flat leaf parsley, coarsely chopped
sea salt and freshly ground black pepper

Serves 4

Bring a saucepan of water to the boil, add the spaghetti, stir and cook for about 9 minutes.

Put the garlic in a bowl and mix in the lemon zest, juice and oil.

Drain the pasta well, then return to the pan, add the lemon mixture, Parmesan, parsley, salt and pepper. Toss well and serve immediately.

Thai noodle salad

Shrimp powder is sold in plastic sachets or jars in Chinese grocers and other Asian markets. It's made from shredded, dried miniature shrimp. Like fish sauce, it acts as a general seasoning. If you can't find it, use extra fish sauce or even soy sauce.

100 g cellophane noodles
1 tablespoon peanut or sunflower oil
1 white onion, diced
2.5 cm fresh ginger, peeled and diced
1 red chilli, deseeded and diced
1 garlic clove, chopped
50 g minced pork
50 g shelled prawns, finely chopped
6 spring onions, sliced
a bunch of coriander, chopped
1 teaspoon fish sauce
1 teaspoon shrimp powder
2 limes, one juiced and the other cut
  into wedges

Serves 4

Soak the cellophane noodles in a bowl of cold water for 10 minutes until soft. Drain well.

Meanwhile, heat the oil in a wok. Add the onion, ginger, chilli and garlic and stir-fry over a medium heat for 5 minutes.

Add the pork and cook for 5 minutes, stirring well to break up the mince. Add the prawns and cook for 3 minutes, then remove from the heat.

Add the spring onions, coriander, fish sauce, shrimp powder, lime juice and drained noodles. Toss well and serve with the lime wedges.

top tip: Try cooked chicken instead of pork and prawns.

Couscous with roasted chicken and vegetables

Remember that your freezer can be a convenient source of good food. Most people don't really use theirs except for ice cubes, ice cream, schnapps and the odd packet of frozen peas or chicken pieces, but that's what's needed for this great meal.

8 small chicken pieces, thawed if frozen
2 onions, cut into wedges
4 garlic cloves
1 aubergine, cut into chunks
2 courgettes, sliced
100 g frozen peas
leaves from a bunch of flat leaf parsley, chopped
125 g couscous
a pinch of saffron threads
olive oil, for roasting (see method)
sea salt and freshly ground black pepper

a heavy-based roasting tin, lightly oiled
Serves 4

Trim the chicken of any excess fat and arrange on the roasting tin. Cook in a preheated oven at 190°C (375°F) Gas 5 for 10 minutes.

Remove the chicken pieces to a plate and set aside. Add the onions, garlic and aubergine to the roasting tin and toss them in the chicken cooking juices, drizzling with a little olive oil if extra lubrication seems necessary.

Return the chicken pieces to the vegetables in the roasting tin and return to the oven to cook for a further 30 minutes, turning halfway through cooking to ensure evening browning. Add the courgettes, peas and parsley to the roasting tin for the final 8 minutes of cooking.

Pour 300 ml boiling water into a saucepan and place over a high heat. Add the couscous and saffron and simmer for 5 minutes. Drain thoroughly, transfer to a large serving dish, season with salt and pepper and fluff up with a fork.

Arrange the cooked chicken and vegetables on top of the couscous, cover and keep warm.

Use a metal spoon to skim off any excess fat from the roasting tin. Place on the stove and heat to simmering. Add 200 ml water, salt and pepper and boil for 4 minutes. Pour over the chicken and couscous and serve.

store cupboard basics

Some weeks seem to whizz by with no time for a shopping trip, but don't fear: it's amazing what great meals can be made from store cupboard staples. Make sure you keep stocked up on essentials such as onions, garlic, olive oil, Parmesan, dried mushrooms, cans of chopped tomatoes and beans, dried pasta and noodles, plus risotto, brown and long-grain rice. Then you'll always be able to prepare a delicious and nutritious dinner for the family or unexpected visitors.

Spaghetti puttanesca

A simple and stylish pasta dish to cook at home, this traditional Italian recipe never seems to lose its appeal. Whenever I find a new Mediterranean delicatessen, I look for special store cupboard items. Anchovies, either in oil or salted, are very good, as are tiny, compact capers. Both these ingredients are real gems that help make this piquant store cupboard dish just as memorable as it can be when eaten on holiday.

300 g dried spaghetti
4 tomatoes, skinned, deseeded and chopped
150 g pitted black olives
75 g canned anchovies, chopped
3 tablespoons capers
leaves from a large bunch of flat leaf parsley, chopped
4 tablespoons olive oil
freshly ground black pepper
75 g Parmesan cheese, grated, to serve
Serves 4

Bring a large saucepan of water to the boil, then add the dried spaghetti, stir well to separate the strands and simmer for 9 minutes.

When the pasta is cooked, drain it thoroughly. Dry the saucepan, then return the spaghetti to the pan and add the tomatoes, olives, anchovies, capers, parsley and olive oil. Season with pepper.

Toss the pasta well and serve with a dish of freshly grated Parmesan for sprinkling.

Spaghetti bolognese

To me, spaghetti bolognese should contain lots of rich tomato sauce and just a little meat. It requires slow simmering to blend all the flavours and make a thick sauce to coat the spaghetti. Children and adults love this recipe. Instead of Parmesan, try serving it with some coarsely grated mature Cheddar cheese, which is my favourite.

4 tablespoons olive oil
2 onions, diced
2 garlic cloves, finely chopped
1 teaspoon dried mixed herbs
400 g good-quality minced beef
2 cans chopped tomatoes, 400 g each
2 tablespoons tomato purée
300 g dried spaghetti
sea salt and freshly ground black pepper
100 g Parmesan or mature Cheddar cheese, grated, to serve
Serves 4

Heat the olive oil in a large saucepan. Add the onions and cook for 5 minutes over a medium heat until softened and translucent. Add the garlic and cook for a further 1 minute.

Stir in the dried mixed herbs and minced beef, stirring thoroughly with a large spoon to break up the mince. Cook for 5 minutes.

Stir in the chopped tomatoes, tomato purée, salt and pepper. Bring the mixture to the boil, then lower the heat and simmer for 45 minutes, stirring occasionally. Check the consistency of the sauce from time to time and add a little water if needed. When cooked, the sauce should be a rich, deep red and thickly coat the back of a spoon.

Bring a large saucepan of water to the boil. Add the spaghetti, stir well to separate the strands and simmer for 9 minutes.

Drain the pasta well and divide between 4 deep serving bowls. Top with the sauce, sprinkle with grated cheese and serve hot.

Classic tomato sauce for pasta

Every cook needs to be able to make this classic tomato sauce. It's good not only with pasta, but great with grilled fish, and can be added to meat casseroles to give extra richness, or spiced with harissa to make a sauce for vegetables and couscous.

4 tablespoons olive oil, plus extra for drizzling
2 onions, chopped
2 garlic cloves, crushed and chopped
3 cans chopped tomatoes, 400 g each
2 teaspoons dried mixed herbs
a pinch of crushed dried chillies
500 g dried spaghetti or penne pasta
sea salt and freshly ground black pepper
100 g Parmesan or mature Cheddar cheese, grated, to serve

Serves 4

Heat the olive oil in a medium saucepan. Add the onion and garlic and cook for 4 minutes over a medium heat until softened and translucent.

Mix in the chopped tomatoes, mixed herbs, dried chillies, salt and pepper. Simmer over a low heat for 25 minutes, stirring occasionally, until the sauce thickens and intensifies in flavour.

In a large saucepan of boiling water, cook the pasta for 9 minutes. Drain well, then toss with 1 tablespoon olive oil.

Add the sauce to the pasta and mix through. Sprinkle with the grated cheese and serve hot.

top tip: You can vary this sauce by including some chopped capers, olives, fresh herbs (torn basil, chopped rosemary, marjoram, thyme, chives, parsley or sorrel), grated courgette, chopped crispy bacon, crumbled goats' cheese or mozzarella – all added just for the last few minutes of cooking.

Curried lentils and spinach

Forget any lentil dishes you may not have enjoyed in the past. This is just so delicious: all the extra flavours bring the lentils to life.

4 tablespoons olive oil
1 onion, diced
1 garlic clove, chopped
1 teaspoon garam masala
1 teaspoon medium-hot curry powder
½ teaspoon crushed cardamom pods
250 g brown lentils
2 tomatoes, skinned and chopped
175 g spinach, cut into ribbons
juice of 1 lemon
sea salt and freshly ground black pepper
Serves 4

Heat the oil in a medium saucepan, add the onion and cook for 5 minutes. Add the garlic, garam masala, curry powder and cardamom, mix well, then cook for 3 minutes.

Add the brown lentils and 500 ml water, bring to the boil, then reduce the heat and simmer for 20 minutes, stirring frequently.

When the lentils are soft, add the tomatoes, spinach, lemon juice, salt and pepper. Stir well and serve hot or warm.

Blue cheese and rosemary polenta mash

Polenta is made from corn, so this comforting Italian dish is a great way to add variety to your carbohydrate intake. Serve it with a tomato and olive salad or, for big appetites, a grilled lamb or pork chop.

150 g quick-cooking polenta grains
50 g butter
2 tablespoons olive oil
100 g Gorgonzola cheese, crumbled
100 g mascarpone cheese
leaves from 1 sprig of rosemary, chopped
sea salt and freshly ground black pepper
Serves 4

Put 600 ml water in a saucepan and heat until simmering. Pour in the polenta and stir vigorously (to prevent it sticking to the bottom of the pan) with a wooden spoon for 5 minutes over a medium heat. The polenta will thicken and stiffen, making the stirring harder, but keep going otherwise you will have lumps.

Add the butter, olive oil and Gorgonzola and mix well, then stir in the mascarpone, rosemary and pepper. Taste and add salt only as necessary, bearing in mind that Gorgonzola is very salty. Mix well and serve.

Rich Tuscan bean soup

4 tablespoons olive oil
150 g pancetta or smoked bacon, diced
1 large onion, chopped
1 garlic clove, crushed and chopped
2 celery stalks, chopped
1 carrot, diced
2 cans chopped tomatoes, 400 g each
1 can cooked butter beans, 400g
½ vegetable or chicken stock cube
freshly ground black pepper

To serve

a bunch of flat leaf parsley, chopped
4 tablespoons olive oil
Serves 4

Heat the oil in a frying pan over medium heat. Add the pancetta and onion and cook for 5 minutes. Add the garlic, celery and carrot and cook for another 5 minutes, mixing well.

Add the tomatoes, butter beans, 250 ml water and a little pepper, then crumble in the stock cube. Bring the mixture to the boil, then lower the heat and simmer for 15 minutes.

Serve in heated soup bowls topped with the chopped parsley and a spoonful of olive oil. Serve with crusty, country-style bread.

Mushroom risotto

They say that a risotto should be constantly stirred, but I don't totally agree that this is necessary. Time is too short. I do stir it frequently, but like to get on with something else in the kitchen at the same time.

1 litre chicken or vegetable stock
50 g dried mushrooms such as chanterelles, morels, shiitakes or porcini
25 g butter
1 tablespoon olive oil
1 garlic clove, crushed and chopped
1 onion, finely chopped
300 g risotto rice
75 ml dry white wine or vermouth
75 g Parmesan cheese, grated, plus 65 g extra, shaved or grated, to serve
sea salt and freshly ground black pepper

Serves 4

Put the stock and dried mushrooms in a saucepan and let soak for 10 minutes. Then slowly heat the stock to simmering point. Strain the mushrooms and return the stock to the saucepan to keep hot.

Melt half the butter with the oil in a large saucepan. Add the garlic and onion and cook over a medium heat until softened and translucent. Add the rice and stir until all the grains are coated with butter and oil.

Add a ladle of hot stock to the rice and mix well. When the rice has absorbed the liquid, add another ladle of stock and stir well. Repeat with the remaining stock, cooking the risotto for 15-20 minutes until all the liquid has been absorbed. Meanwhile, chop the mushrooms into smaller pieces as necessary.

Add the soaked mushrooms, white wine or vermouth, the remaining butter and the grated Parmesan to the risotto. Season to taste with salt and pepper and mix gently over the heat for 2 minutes. Serve with a separate dish of the shaved or grated cheese to sprinkle over the top.

Salade Niçoise

One taste of this and you will quickly forget every other Salade Niçoise you have ever eaten.

400 g tuna steak, quartered
4 medium new potatoes, cooked and sliced
4 tomatoes, skinned and cut into wedges
100 g cooked French beans, trimmed and halved
1 red onion, sliced
4 baby lettuce, such as Little Gem, quartered lengthways
4 hard-boiled eggs, peeled and halved
4 anchovies, cut into long strips
12 black olives, pitted
a bunch of flat leaf parsley, coarsely chopped
4 tablespoons olive oil
4 tablespoons balsamic vinegar

sea salt and freshly ground black pepper
1 lemon, cut into wedges, to serve
Serves 4

Heat a stove-top grill pan or an overhead grill, add the tuna and and cook for 1–2 minutes each side. Remove from the heat and set aside in a warm place.

Put the cooked sliced potatoes in a bowl with the tomato wedges, beans, onion, lettuce and eggs. Add the anchovies, olives, parsley, olive oil, balsamic vinegar, salt and pepper. Mix carefully.

Put the tuna on top of the salad and serve with wedges of lemon. Alternatively, the traditional way to serve this salad is to arrange groups of the ingredients on a large platter, then drizzle with the olive oil and vinegar.

top tip: To peel tomatoes, bring a saucepan of water to the boil, cut a cross in the skin at the base of each tomato, then plunge them into the boiling water for just 20 seconds. Drain, then peel the skin away when the tomatoes are cool enough to handle.

Risotto primavera

Risottos are very personal. Some like them very wet with the rice thoroughly cooked, others prefer a drier texture, or the rice still quite crunchy on the inside. My preference is for the rice to be slightly nutty and just wet enough to bind all the ingredients.

1 litre chicken or vegetable stock
100 g butter
3 tablespoons olive oil
1 onion, diced
1 garlic clove, chopped
275 g arborio or carnaroli rice
625 g mixed green vegetables, such as asparagus, broad beans, dwarf beans, flat beans, runner beans, green cabbage, peas or spinach, all chopped into evenly-sized pieces.
75 ml dry vermouth or white wine
a bunch of flat leaf parsley, chopped
125 g Parmesan cheese, freshly grated
sea salt and freshly ground black pepper
Serves 4

Pour the stock into a small saucepan and heat to simmering point.

Heat the butter and olive oil in a large saucepan. Add the onion and garlic and cook over a low heat for 5 minutes until softened and translucent.

Add the rice, stirring with a wooden spoon to coat the grains thoroughly with butter and oil (this helps to make the risotto creamy).

Add a ladle of stock to the rice, mix well and let simmer. When the liquid has almost evaporated, add another ladle of stock to the saucepan and stir thoroughly until it bubbles away. Continue, stirring the risotto as often as possible and adding more stock as needed.

After the risotto has been cooking for 12 minutes, add all the vegetables and mix well. Add the remaining stock, vermouth or white wine, salt and pepper. Cook, stirring, for a further 4–5 minutes, then mix in the chopped parsley and grated Parmesan cheese. Serve immediately.

supper on a tray

Sitting in a comfy chair and eating from a tray is one of the unsung pleasures of home life – indulgent, yet thoroughly casual. Big bowls of hearty food are best here, served with a cool drink and a smattering of drama courtesy of your favourite soap.

comfort food

These recipes are for those days when you need an inside tummy hug. Choose from a cuddly classic pie, its rich steaming filling topped with home-made crumbly pastry, or a salad of silky avocado, tender chickpeas and spinach bound together with creamy dressing, or that most wicked of puddings, banoffi – even the name is comforting to say.

Steak and mushroom pie

Nothing beats a good home-made pie with tender pieces of meat in a delicious gravy. This one is topped with crisp suet pastry.

Filling

3 tablespoons olive oil
2 onions, chopped
750 g braising steak, cubed
200 g button mushrooms
1 tablespoon flour
½ teaspoon dried mixed herbs
1 teaspoon Worcestershire sauce
1 teaspoon English mustard, or Dijon
400 ml beef stock
sea salt and freshly ground black pepper

Suet pastry

250 g self-raising flour
125 g shredded suet or shortening

a 1.2 litre pie dish
Serves 4

To make the filling, heat the olive oil in a large frying pan, add the onions and fry until softened and translucent. Transfer to a plate.

Add a little more oil to the pan if needed, then add the meat and sauté until browned and sealed.

Add the mushrooms and fry for about 5 minutes, then sprinkle in the flour and mix well to absorb all the oil.

Return the onions to the pan and add the mixed herbs, Worcestershire sauce, mustard, salt and pepper. Slowly pour in the stock, blending well. Bring to the boil, then lower the heat and simmer the mixture for 1½ hours.

When the meat is almost cooked, make the pastry. Sift the flour into a bowl, add the suet or shortening, salt and pepper and mix well.

Add about 5 tablespoons water and mix with a round-bladed knife until the mixture forms a dough. A little more water may be needed, but take care not to add too much as it will make the pastry difficult to handle.

Transfer the cooked meat to the pie dish, and set aside to cool.

Roll out the pastry to a disc larger than the pie dish. Wet the lip of the dish, then cut thin strips of pastry from the trimmings and press onto the lip. Dampen this pastry lip. Lay the rolled pastry over the pie and flute the edge with your fingers to seal. Trim and make a small hole in the centre.

Bake in a preheated oven at 220°C (425°F) Gas 7 for 35 minutes, until golden brown.

top tip: Suet pastry is best for savoury pies as it is richer and more filling than a light flaky pastry. For vegetarian pies you can buy vegetarian suet.

Avocado and chickpea salad

This is a fresh and yet instant meal for lazy evenings. When buying avocados, make sure that they are slightly soft to the touch and blemish-free.

2 eggs
250 g baby spinach, sliced into ribbons
1 can chickpeas, 400 g, rinsed and drained
2 ripe avocados, halved, pitted, peeled and sliced
2 teaspoons sweet Spanish paprika
bread such as ciabatta or focaccia, to serve

Creamy chive dressing

juice of 1 lemon
3 tablespoons milk
2 tablespoons fromage frais or Greek yoghurt
a bunch of chives, chopped
sea salt and freshly ground black pepper
Serves 4

Put the eggs in a small saucepan of water, bring to the boil and cook until hard-boiled, 8–9 minutes. Drain, cool, shell, cut into quarters and set aside.

To make the dressing, put the lemon juice in a bowl with the milk, fromage frais or yoghurt and chopped chives. Season generously with salt and pepper and stir until smooth.

Put the spinach, chickpeas, avocados and eggs in a bowl. Sprinkle with the sweet paprika, then spoon over the dressing. Serve with fresh bread.

Tarte Tatin

This French upside-down tart of caramelized apples was invented by the Tatin sisters, who had a hotel in Lamotte-Beuvran. Maxim's in Paris took it into the culinary mainstream and still serves it today, as do a great many restaurants around the world. Chefs like to experiment with alternative fruits such as bananas, clementines and mango, but I think apple remains the best.

100 g caster sugar
40 g butter
5 eating apples, peeled, cored and quartered
cream or ice cream, to serve

Pastry
150 g plain flour
100 g butter
25 g caster sugar
2 egg yolks

a 20 cm ovenproof frying pan
Serves 4

To make the pastry, put the flour in a mixing bowl, then rub in the butter with your fingertips until the mixture looks like breadcrumbs. Stir in the caster sugar.

Place the egg yolks in a small bowl and beat lightly with a fork. Add the yolks to the pastry and mix using a round-bladed knife until the dough binds together and forms a ball.

Dust your hands with flour. Working quickly, put the dough on a lightly floured work surface and knead until smooth. Wrap in clingfilm and chill for 20 minutes.

To make the tarte, melt the sugar and butter together in the frying pan over a medium heat until syrupy. Add the quartered apples and cook for a further 10–15 minutes. Remove from the heat when the apples are golden and the syrup is thick and smells of caramel.

Put the pastry on a lightly floured surface and roll out to a circle slightly larger than the frying pan. Lay the pastry over the apples and tuck the edges of the pastry around the sides of the pan.

Transfer the frying pan to a preheated oven at 200°C (400°F) Gas 6 and cook for 40 minutes; check after 20 minutes and reduce the heat if the tart seems to be browning too quickly.

Remove the tart from the oven. Put a heatproof plate on top of the frying pan and quickly turn it upside down, taking care not to drip any of the hot juices on your skin. Lift the frying pan off the pie – the pastry will be underneath and the caramelized apples on top.

Slice and serve warm with cream or ice cream.

Banoffi pie

Very rich and delicious, banoffi pie is only for those with an ardent sweet tooth. I boil up several cans of condensed milk at once, then keep them in the cupboard until needed.

1 can condensed milk, 225 g
275 g digestive biscuits
100 g butter
3 bananas
200 ml double cream
30 g good-quality dark chocolate (70 per cent cocoa solids)

a 20 cm loose-based flan tin
Serves 4

Put the unopened can of condensed milk in a large saucepan. Cover with water, bring to the boil, then reduce the heat and simmer for 3 hours. Check the water level from time to time and top up as necessary. Let cool overnight.

Put the digestive biscuits in a blender or food processor and whizz until crushed.

Melt the butter in a small saucepan. Add the biscuit crumbs and mix well. Pour the buttered crumbs into the flan dish and spread evenly over the bottom and up the sides to form a pie crust. Place in the refrigerator to set.

Open the cooled can of condensed milk to reveal the sticky caramel. Spoon it into the pie crust and spread out evenly.

Slice the bananas and lay them on top of the caramel. Whip the cream in a large bowl until soft peaks form, then use it to cover the pie.

Grate the chocolate and sprinkle it over the cream to decorate. Refrigerate until ready to serve.

top tip: When flipping the cooked tarte Tatin out of the frying pan onto a plate, be sure to protect your hands and arms by wearing proper oven gloves. The faster you turn the pan over, the less likely it is that the hot cooking juices will escape and burn you, but keep a firm grip on the frying pan and plate.

one-pot meals

Bouillabaisse

Buy only the freshest and best quality fish for this classic Mediterranean dish. From the white fish family you can choose from bream, cod, halibut, monkfish, red mullet, snapper, sole or whiting. If using an oily fish, salmon is the preferred variety. Good bouillabaisse also features other seafood such as prawns, mussels, and clams. If you're feeling rich, you can also include a lobster.

Ask the fishmonger to clean, scale and fillet the fish and keep all the bones to make the stock. Make sure he removes all the scales (this is especially important for snapper).

100 ml olive oil
1 large onion, diced
2 leeks, finely sliced
2 garlic cloves, crushed and chopped
1 small bulb of fennel, diced
750 ml passata
900 ml fish stock (see below)
a sprig of thyme
1 fresh bay leaf
a pinch of saffron threads
2 kg fish and shellfish, cleaned, scaled and
  filleted, heads and bones reserved
sea salt and freshly ground black pepper
warm crusty bread, to serve

Fish stock
fish bones and heads
1 onion, sliced
1 carrot, sliced
1 leek, sliced
5 sprigs of parsley
1 fresh bay leaf
Serves 4

To make the fish stock, put all the fish bones, heads and the shells of any seafood in a large saucepan or stockpot. Cover with water, add the onion, carrot, leek, parsley sprigs, bay leaf, salt and pepper. Bring the mixture to the boil and simmer for just 20 minutes, skimming off the foam from time to time.

Strain the stock and reserve 800 ml to use in this recipe - you can cool and freeze any extra for use in another dish.

To make the bouillabaisse, heat the olive oil in a large frying pan. Add the onion, leeks, garlic and fennel and sauté the vegetables for 5 minutes without letting them brown.

Add the passata, thyme, bay leaf, saffron, fish stock, salt and pepper. Bring to the boil, reduce the heat and simmer for 10 minutes.

Add the cleaned pieces of fish and shellfish and cook for 4 minutes.

Carefully lift out the fish fillets and shellfish and divide between 4 large bowls. Ladle over the rich tomato liquid and serve with warm crusty bread.

Spaghetti carbonara

Easy but truly delicious, this Italian classic never seems to lose its popularity.

1 tablespoon olive oil
200 g smoked bacon, cut into strips
1 garlic clove, crushed and chopped
300 g dried spaghetti
6 tablespoons double cream
4 egg yolks
100 g Parmesan cheese, freshly grated
sea salt and freshly ground black pepper
Serves 4

Heat the oil in a large saucepan, add the bacon and cook over a medium heat for 3 minutes. Add the garlic and cook for a further minute. Remove from the pan and set aside.

Fill the pan with boiling water from the kettle. Add the dried spaghetti, stirring well to stop it sticking together. Return to the boil, then reduce the heat and simmer for 9 minutes.

When cooked, drain the spaghetti and return it to the pan. Add the cooked bacon mixture, cream, egg yolks, Parmesan, salt and pepper. Mix well over the heat for 1-2 minutes to coat the pasta in the sauce and cook the eggs.

Serve immediately in warm bowls.

top tip: If you prefer not to eat meat, you can replace the bacon in this sauce with a variety of mushrooms, such as chestnut, field and button.

Steaming bowls of delicious goodness, one-pot meals are comforting and easy, with the added bonus that there is only one pan to wash afterwards. These wonderful dishes – good for adults and children – take their inspiration from around the world, from the Med to South-east Asia, proving that simple home cooking need never be dull.

Butternut and cashew nut soup

The colour and velvety-smooth flavour of this soup make it a winner with the whole family. For special occasions, serve with Parmesan wafers (page 137).

4 tablespoons olive oil
50 g butter
1 onion, chopped
1 butternut squash, about 1 kg, peeled, deseeded and
    coarsely chopped
1 teaspoon medium curry powder
200 ml milk
125 g cashew nuts, coarsely chopped
sea salt and freshly ground black pepper

Serves 4

Heat the olive oil and butter in a large saucepan over a medium heat. Add the onion and cook for 5 minutes until softened and translucent.

Add the chopped butternut, curry powder, salt and pepper, then cook for 5 minutes.

Pour in 500 ml water and milk, then bring the mixture to the boil, lower the heat and simmer for 30 minutes.

Add the cashew nuts and cool briefly. Working in batches if necessary, transfer the soup to a blender or food processor and purée until smooth and thick. Alternatively, use a hand-held blender and purée in the saucepan.

Reheat the soup as necessary. Taste and adjust the seasoning to your liking, then serve hot.

Green bean and herb broth

I prefer this soup served on its own – it makes a perfect light meal. If you need a dish that is a little more filling, add some pasta or noodles at the same time as the stock. The vegetables and herbs in this soup need only quick, light cooking to bring out their delicate flavours.

4 tablespoons olive oil
1 onion, very finely sliced
1 garlic clove, crushed and chopped
1 litre vegetable stock
200 g French beans, cut into 2.5 cm pieces
200 g runner beans, cut into 2.5 cm pieces
200 g shelled broad beans, peeled

sea salt and freshly ground black pepper
a bunch of chervil, coarsely chopped
a bunch of dill, coarsely chopped
Serves 4

Heat the olive oil in a large saucepan or stockpot. Add the sliced onion and cook over a low heat for 10 minutes without letting it brown. Add the garlic and cook gently for a further 5 minutes.

Pour in the stock and add some salt and pepper. Bring to the boil and simmer for 5 minutes.

Add all the beans to the soup and simmer for 4 minutes, then add the chopped fresh herbs and cook for a further 2 minutes only. Serve immediately.

When I want something light but flavoursome, filling but not too heavy, a generous bowl of quickly made noodle stir-fry or a pure and delicate vegetable broth is the perfect choice. Healthy, fast and delicious – what more could you want?

Vegetable noodle stir-fry

When making this dish, prepare all the vegetables in advance, so the stir-fry can be quickly and easily put together. Don't overcook the vegetables – they are better when crunchy and brightly coloured. You can change the vegetables according to what's in your fridge or what your children like, but always use the onion, garlic, ginger and chilli.

4 tablespoons vegetable oil
1 garlic clove, crushed and chopped
5 cm fresh ginger, diced
1 onion, finely sliced
1 chilli, finely chopped
125 g thin noodles, such as egg noodles
2 pak choi, about 250 g, roughly chopped
1 leek, cut into strips
75 g beansprouts, rinsed and trimmed
75 g mushrooms, sliced
3 tablespoons soy sauce
juice of 1 lime
a bunch of coriander, chopped
Serves 4

Heat the oil in a wok. Add the garlic, ginger, onion and chilli and cook over a medium heat, stirring constantly.

Bring a large saucepan of water to the boil. Add the noodles and cook for 1 minute if fresh or 3 minutes if dried. Drain thoroughly.

Add the pak choi, leek, beansprouts and mushrooms to the wok and stir-fry for 2–3 minutes.

Add the soy sauce, lime juice and noodles and use 2 spoons to mix the vegetables and noodles together. Top with the chopped coriander and serve immediately in bowls with chopsticks instead of cutlery.

Thai meatballs and noodles

Here is a lovely and warming noodle broth with tasty chicken meatballs. The blend of flavours is quite heavenly in this one-pot dish and I'm sure you will want to make it often. If you don't like very hot chillies, use a milder variety, such as jalapeño, instead of the fiery bird's eye chilli.

500 g chicken, finely minced
1 small onion, diced
5 cm fresh ginger, peeled and chopped
2 bird's eye chillies, deseeded and diced
2 garlic cloves, chopped
600 ml chicken stock
300 g noodles, such as egg noodles
sea salt
a bunch of coriander, chopped, to serve
Serves 4

Put the chicken, onion, ginger, chillies, garlic and some salt in a bowl and mix with your hands (this is easier than using a spoon). Divide the mixture into 16 equal portions and roll into balls using wet hands.

Place the chicken stock in a large saucepan or pot and bring to the boil. Carefully add the chicken meatballs, reduce the heat and simmer for 10 minutes.

Add the noodles and push down to submerge them in the chicken stock. Cook for 4–8 minutes, or according to the packet instructions.

Spoon the noodles, meatballs and broth into large bowls and serve topped with the chopped coriander.

top tip: Finely mincing the chicken helps bind the meatballs together. Other meats such as pork or beef or minced white fish or prawns can be used to make these dumplings.

Heat the olive oil in a paella pan or large frying pan. Add the onion, garlic and chorizo. Cook over a low heat until the onion is softened and translucent, about 5 minutes.

Add the chicken pieces and cook for about 5 minutes on each side until lightly browned.

Add the rice, saffron and stock to the pan and mix well. Bring the mixture to the boil, reduce the heat and simmer for 15 minutes, stirring so the rice doesn't stick to the base of the pan. Add more stock if needed.

Add the white wine, mussels, prawns, squid, salt and pepper. Cover with a lid or piece of foil and cook, without stirring, for a further 8–10 minutes.

Juice 1 lemon and cut the other into wedges. Stir the juice into the paella. Top with the chopped parsley and serve from the pan with lemon wedges on the side.

Steamed syrup pudding

An easy-to-make winter classic, this pudding is always a winner. You could omit the syrup and use the same volume of honey, jam, lemon curd or a little chopped stem ginger.

250 g butter, softened
250 g caster sugar
3 eggs
375 g self-raising flour
50 ml milk
4 tablespoons golden syrup
vanilla ice cream, to serve

a 1 litre pudding basin, buttered
Serves 4

Put the butter and sugar in a medium mixing bowl and beat with a wooden spoon until pale and creamy. Add the eggs one at a time and beat until blended.

Sift the flour over the egg mixture and, using a large metal spoon, carefully fold in the flour. Add the milk and continue folding the mixture until smooth.

Pour the golden syrup into the buttered pudding basin. Spoon the sponge mixture on top. Cover with baking parchment and secure with kitchen string.

Sit the pudding basin in a large saucepan. Pour in boiling water from the kettle until it comes about halfway up the sides of the basin. Cover and simmer gently for 1 hour, topping up with more boiling water as necessary.

Carefully remove the pudding basin from the saucepan and peel off the paper. Place a large serving plate on top of the basin, then turn the pudding over, giving it a gentle shake to release it from the mould.

Cut the pudding at the table and serve on small plates or in bowls, accompanied by the ice cream.

Paella

This wonderful Spanish dish is very easy to make and a joy to eat. Don't be put off by the long list of ingredients – they are all readily available from your local supermarket. On special occasions, serve the paella with a mixed leaf salad, followed by fresh fruit and Spanish cheeses for a very stylish meal (and a happy cook).

2 tablespoons olive oil
1 onion, diced
2 garlic cloves, crushed and chopped
100 g chorizo sausage, thickly sliced
4 skinned chicken pieces, trimmed
200 g long grain rice
a large pinch of saffron strands
600 ml chicken stock
250 ml white wine
12 mussels, cleaned
8 large prawns
100 g squid, cleaned and cut into rings
sea salt and freshly ground black pepper
2 lemons
a bunch of flat leaf parsley, chopped
Serves 4

smart drinks and finger food

The idea of attempting a glamorous and sophisticated drinks party at home sends most of us into a panic and often results in a quick phone call to the caterers. Trust me: you can invite a select few people and serve any of the following recipes for a sensational party that will be long remembered for the style and elegance of its drinks, food and company.

Brazen martini

50 ml Bison vodka
25 ml Parfait d' Amour violet liqueur
ice cubes, for shaking

a cocktail shaker
Makes 1

Fill the shaker with ice cubes. Add the vodka and violet liqueur and shake until well blended and chilled. Strain the mixture into a cocktail glass and serve.

Blueberry martini

8-10 blueberries
50 ml vodka
25 ml crème de cassis
ice cubes, for shaking

a cocktail shaker
Makes 1

Put the blueberries in the shaker and crush them with a pestle or the back of a spoon.

Fill the shaker with ice and add the vodka and crème de cassis. Shake until well blended and chilled. Use a fine sieve to strain the mixture into a cocktail glass. Serve.

Parmesan wafers

These wafers taste fantastic and are so easy to make – yes, there really is only one ingredient!

275 g Parmesan cheese, grated

a baking sheet, lined with baking parchment
Makes 20

Pile teaspoons of the grated Parmesan on the paper-lined baking sheet and flatten gently to give equal rounds.

Bake in a preheated oven at 190°C (375°F) Gas 5 for 5 minutes – the cheese will melt, bubble and turn golden.

Remove the paper from the baking sheet with the biscuits still on it. Replace with another sheet of paper and repeat with the remaining cheese.

When the wafers are cool, remove and store in an airtight container until needed.

top tip: To ring the changes, add a little coarsely ground black pepper, some chopped rosemary or finely chopped pine nuts to the cheese.

Avruga baby baked potatoes

Avruga, like little black pearls, is herring roe and has a lovely, mellow, slightly smoky flavour. If unavailable, use other fish eggs such as salmon (keta) or trout, or splash out on fine caviar.

10 baby potatoes
½ head of celery
125 g sour cream
100 g avruga, keta, trout roe or caviar

a baking sheet, oiled
Makes 10 of each

Put the potatoes on the baking sheet and cook in a preheated oven at 180°C (350°F) Gas 4 for 15 minutes. Remove and let cool for 10 minutes.

Cut small, deep crosses in the potatoes, then squeeze to open out slightly. Spoon a small amount of sour cream in each potato and top with a spoonful of avruga.

Cut the celery into 7 cm lengths and put a spoonful of avruga at the end of each one. Serve.

top tip: If you're catering for a lot of people, serve the soured cream and avruga in small bowls with spoons. Cut the cooked baby potatoes and squeeze open, but let guests fill their own.

Sea breeze

50 ml vodka
125 ml cranberry juice
50 ml grapefruit juice
ice cubes, to serve
Makes 1

Fill a highball glass with ice, add the vodka, then the fruit juices, stir and serve.

Cosmopolitan

25 ml Absolut-citron vodka
25 ml Cointreau
50 ml cranberry juice
25 ml freshly squeezed lime juice
ice cubes, for shaking

a cocktail shaker
Makes 1

Fill the shaker with ice cubes. Add the alcohol and juices and shake until well blended and chilled. Strain into a cocktail glass and serve.

French 75

25 ml gin
25 ml freshly squeezed lemon juice
a dash of sugar syrup
75 ml chilled champagne, plus extra to serve
ice cubes, for shaking

a cocktail shaker
Makes 1

Put the gin, lemon juice and sugar syrup in the cocktail shaker. Add the ice and shake.

Pour into a champagne flute, add the champagne and top up with more champagne before serving.

Pimm's cocktail

Use your own selection of fresh fruit, but orange, cucumber and mint are traditional.

50 ml Pimm's No. 1
225 ml lemonade
1 slice lemon
2 sprigs of mint
2 slices cucumber, cut lengthways
ice cubes, to serve
Makes 1

Fill a highball glass with ice and add each of the ingredients in turn. Serve cold.

Crispy noodles

These are also called *mee krob* and always popular, so be sure to make plenty.

sunflower oil, for deep-frying, plus
    1 tablespoon extra for stir-frying
50 g rice vermicelli
1 onion, finely diced
1 garlic clove, crushed and chopped
2.5 cm fresh ginger, peeled and diced
1 fresh red chilli, diced
a bunch of coriander, chopped
a bunch of chives, chopped
2 mini lettuces, such as Little Gem
Makes 20

Fill a wok one-third full of oil and heat. To test if the oil is hot enough to begin cooking, add a piece of vermicelli: it should puff up immediately, if it sinks to the bottom heat the oil a little more.

Add the vermicelli in small handfuls, turning it with tongs to help it puff up evenly, then remove to a plate lined with crumpled kitchen paper. Pour the oil into a heatproof container.

Wipe out the wok and return to the heat. Add 1 tablespoon oil, then the onion, garlic, ginger and chilli. Stir-fry for 5 minutes.

Turn off the heat, add the cooked noodles to the wok and mix well. Stir in the herbs.

Break the lettuce leaves away from the stem. Fill them with spoonfuls of the noodle mixture, arrange on a plate to serve.

Goats' cheese and pepper crostini

Buy a smooth and creamy goats' cheese that has no rind. They are usually sold in a pot.

1 thin French breadstick (ficelle)
150 g fresh creamy goats' milk cheese
4 roasted red peppers, peeled
20 spears Thai asparagus, cooked and refreshed in cold water
sea salt and black pepper
olive oil, for brushing

a baking sheet
Serves 20

To make the crostini, slice the bread diagonally into 20 thin slices. Brush with olive oil, then add salt and pepper. Cook in a preheated oven at 190°C (375°F) Gas 5 for 5 minutes until golden.

Arrange the crostini on a plate and spread with goats' cheese. Cut the roasted peppers into thin strips. Arrange a strip of pepper and a spear of asparagus on each crostini and serve.

Mojito

1 lime, cut into 16 pieces
enough mint tips to half-fill the glass
2 teaspoons sugar
50 ml dark rum
crushed ice, to serve
soda water, to taste (optional)

Makes 1

Put the lime and mint into an old-fashioned glass, then sprinkle with sugar. Using a pestle or the back of a spoon, crush the lime, mint and sugar together until the sugar has completely dissolved.

Fill the glass with crushed ice, add the rum and stir briefly. Add soda water to taste if desired.

Chinese duck forks

These irresistible duck morsels are sweet, delicious and look wonderful. Serve them skewered on little forks, or on some Chinese porcelain spoons (which don't cost much, but look terrific).

1 duck breast, skinned
3 spring onions, cut into 5 cm pieces, then finely sliced lengthways
10 cm cucumber, peeled, deseeded, cut into 5 cm pieces, then finely sliced lengthways

Chinese marinade

2 tablespoons soy sauce
2 tablespoons dry sherry

1 tablespoon caster sugar
2 whole star anise
5 cm fresh ginger, chopped
4 tablespoons plum sauce

12 forks or Chinese porcelain spoons
Serves 12

Put all the marinade ingredients in a small non-stick pan and heat to simmering point.

Add the duck breast and simmer very gently for 6 minutes on each side. Remove from the heat, cover and cool. When cool, slice the duck very thinly crossways. Reserve the marinade.

Lay out the sliced duck breast, put a few spring onion and cucumber strips at one end and roll up tightly into parcels. Push onto the forks or lay in the Chinese spoons, drizzle with a little of the reserved marinade and serve.

Mexican prawn wraps

These canapés are visually stunning. The prawns can be replaced with chicken, rare beef or grated fresh vegetables such as carrots and radishes. A long, cool Mojito is the perfect accompaniment to these wraps.

2 flour tortillas, 20 cm diameter

Salsa

1 jalapeño chilli, deseeded and finely diced
½ red onion, finely diced
1 garlic clove, finely diced
2 tomatoes, skinned, deseeded and diced
3 tablespoons sour cream
sea salt and freshly ground black pepper

Filling

½ avocado, peeled and sliced
juice of ½ lime
75 g cooked and peeled prawns
a small bunch of rocket, about 50 g

makes 20

To make the salsa, put all the ingredients in a bowl and stir well.

Heat the tortillas in a dry frying pan, then transfer to a large chopping board. Divide the salsa between them and spread out evenly. Top with avocado and sprinkle with a little lime juice. Scatter the prawns and rocket over the tortillas.

Roll up tightly and wrap in clingfilm, twisting the ends to secure. Chill for 30 minutes, then slice each roll into 10 pieces and arrange on a platter.

Lobby dazzler

3–4 kumquats, quartered
2 teaspoons sugar
50 ml Absolut-kurant vodka
crushed ice, to serve
Makes 1

Put the kumquats in an old-fashioned glass and sprinkle with sugar. Using a
pestle or the back of a spoon, crush the kumquat and sugar together until the
sugar completely dissolves and all the fruit juice is released.

Fill the glass with crushed ice, add the vodka and stir briefly before serving.

party time

Invite lots of friends, fill a table with food and drink and let people help themselves. Sounds easy, and yes it can be – but to me the food is all-important. I have put together a great-tasting feast for you here, so pile the plates high, put all the cutlery, napkins and glasses on the table and let the party begin.

It takes organization followed by more organization to throw a memorable party, but it can be achieved with ease if you follow these helpful tips. Start with a date, venue, list of friends and style of party, then send the invitations.

Keep the food simple and limit the courses. Choose dishes that can be made in advance and presented as a buffet so that you need not spend the evening locked in the kitchen. I always supplement the cooking with a good salad, ripe soft cheese, breads and a large platter of prepared fresh fruit placed on the table at the end of the meal for guests to help themselves.

Enjoy decorating your space with items related to the theme of the party. Empty a room, fill it with rugs, a large low table, soft cushions, scented candles, maybe some rose petals scattered over the table. Finally, open your doors and party!

top tip: Shop wisely at a good deli to enhance your menu. Buy antipasto vegetables to add to the salad, select a fine cheese board and don't skimp on the artisan-made breads.

menu

Artichoke and cheese tart

Peppered beef with
watercress salad

Tiramisu

Cabernet Sauvignon

Artichoke and cheese tart

This flexible and remarkably easy tart can be topped with all sorts of vegetables and any of your favourite cheeses – the combinations are limitless, so don't hesitate to experiment.

2 packets ready-made puff pastry, 500 g
5 roasted peppers, cut into 2.5 cm strips
3 jars artichoke hearts in oil, 290 g each
6 medium onions, sliced
500 g baby leeks, trimmed and washed
500 g cheese, coarsely grated or crumbled
1 egg yolk, beaten
3–4 tablespoons extra virgin olive oil
sea salt andfreshly ground black pepper

2 baking sheets, lightly oiled
Serves 20

Roll out each packet of pastry and place one piece on each baking sheet. Prick all over with a fork, then bake in a preheated oven at 180°C (350°F) Gas 4 for 20 minutes.

Put the roasted peppers in a large bowl with the artichokes, onions, leeks, cheese, salt and pepper. Mix well.

Remove the cooked pastry from the oven, then brush all over with the beaten egg yolk.

Divide the filling between the pastry sheets and spread out evenly. Return the tarts to the oven and bake for a further 30 minutes.

Serve hot or at room temperature, lightly drizzled with a little extra virgin olive oil.

top tip: This tart can be part-baked one day ahead. Cook the pastry, cover with clingfilm and store it in an airtight container until needed. Mix all the topping ingredients, cover and chill. Then assemble on the day – if you make it completely the day before, you run the risk of the pastry becoming soggy.

Peppered beef with watercress salad

Fillet is the finest cut of beef but if you need something a little more economical, try roasting a piece of sirloin or fore rib.

6 egg whites
2.5 kg fillet or rump steak, well trimmed.
6 tablespoons coarsely crushed peppercorns
4 tablespoons mixed mustard seeds
1 kg vine tomatoes
6 bunches of watercress, about 100 g each
500 g mixed lettuce leaves, torn into small pieces
30 hard-boiled quails' eggs, halved

Orange dressing

1 tablespoon caster sugar
juice and zest of 3 oranges
2 tablespoons balsamic vinegar
3 tablespoons clear honey
2 garlic cloves, crushed and chopped

200 ml sunflower oil
sea salt and freshly ground black pepper

a roasting tin
a baking sheet, lightly oiled
Serves 20

Lightly whisk the egg whites in a large bowl for 2 minutes. Add the beef and turn until it is well coated with the egg whites.

Mix the peppercorns and mustard on a flat plate, then roll the beef in the mixture to make a crust.

Put the tomatoes on the baking sheet and cook in a preheated oven at 190°C (375°F) Gas 5 for 1 hour. Meanwhile, pour the olive oil into the roasting tin and heat in the oven.

When the oil is hot, add the beef, turning to coat in the hot oil. Roast at the top of the oven for 45 minutes for rare meat, 1 hour for medium and 1½ hours for well done. Remove the tomatoes from the oven when cooked and set aside to cool. Set the meat aside to rest for 10 minutes.

When ready to serve, mix the watercress with the other leaves and put on a serving platter with the tomatoes and quails' eggs.

To make the dressing, put the sugar in a bowl with the orange zest and juice, vinegar, honey, garlic and some salt and pepper. Whisk in the oil with a fork or hand-held blender.

Slice the beef into thin strips and arrange on top of the salad. Just before serving, stir the dressing and drizzle it over the salad.

Robust food with chunky textures and distinct flavours is best for lively parties and suits whatever kind of alcohol your friends are drinking. Make sure you offer plenty of water and other non-alcoholic drinks too so that all guests feel welcome.

Tiramisu

Foolproof and very quick to prepare, tiramisu is a wonderful pudding to serve a large group of people – it can be made in advance, doesn't need cooking or heating and tastes so delicious that it is universally welcomed. I like to make it with amaretti and present it in 20 groovy glasses instead of one very large serving bowl.

50 amaretti biscuits, crushed
200 ml Kahlúa (coffee liqueur)
6 tablespoons brandy
100 ml strong black coffee
1 kg mascarpone cheese
12 eggs separated
100 g caster sugar, sifted
250 g dark chocolate, grated, or 4 tablespoons cocoa powder

20 glasses or a 30 cm square serving dish
Serves 20

Arrange a quarter of the crushed amaretti biscuits at the bottom of the glasses or serving dish. Mix the Kahlúa in a small bowl with the brandy and coffee and pour a quarter of this mixture over the crushed biscuits.

Put the mascarpone, egg yolks and caster sugar in a bowl and beat until smooth and lump-free. Put the egg whites in a separate bowl, whisk until stiff, then fold into the mascarpone mixture.

Spoon a quarter of the mixture over the biscuits, then repeat the layers 3 times, finishing with a layer of mascarpone mixture.

Sprinkle the chocolate or cocoa over the top of the tiramisu and refrigerate overnight. Serve chilled or at room temperature.

top tip: Instead of topping the tiramisu with grated chocolate, melt the chocolate in a plastic bag tied securely to close. Make a small hole in one corner and pipe 20 squiggles onto baking parchment. Let set, then stick the chocolate shapes upright into the individual tiramisus.

supper for friends

Mulled wine

Warm your house and make your friends' hearts glow with this beautiful spicy drink also known as *glühwein*. If making it for a big party, add more wine and sugar to the pan as the evening wears on.

2 bottles red wine, 750 ml each
8 whole cloves
2 oranges
3 tablespoons brown sugar
5 cm fresh ginger, peeled and chopped
1 cinnamon stick
½ teaspoon freshly grated nutmeg

Serves 4

Pour the red wine into a medium saucepan. Insert the cloves in the oranges, then cut each orange into quarters. Add to the pan, together with the sugar, ginger, cinnamon and nutmeg.

Heat the mixture to simmering point and simmer for 8–10 minutes, then serve hot.

Green chicken curry

A great meal to serve for all occasions, this dish will improve with time so make it the night before, reheat well and add the herbs just before serving. The coconut milk gives a beautiful silky quality to the fragrant sauce.

4 tablespoons vegetable oil
1 onion, sliced
5 cm fresh ginger, peeled and sliced
2 garlic cloves, crushed and chopped
2 stalks lemongrass, finely sliced
2 green chillies, chopped
8 skinless chicken pieces
2 teaspoon medium-hot curry powder
4 kaffir lime leaves, or a strip of lime peel
200 ml coconut milk
sea salt and freshly ground black pepper

To serve

a bunch of basil leaves, torn
a bunch of coriander, chopped
steamed Thai rice

Serves 4

Heat the oil in a large saucepan. Add the onion, ginger, garlic, lemongrass and chillies and sauté over a low heat for 10 minutes.

Add the chicken and cook for 5 minutes to seal on all sides. Mix in the curry powder, kaffir lime leaves or lime peel, salt and pepper.

Stir in the coconut milk and 200 ml boiling water, then cover and simmer for 40 minutes. Do not boil or the coconut milk will curdle.

Spoon the curry into a serving dish, top with the basil and coriander and serve with Thai rice.

You've known each other for years and see them often, but still there are few people you'd rather cook for. Supper could be two fun courses served at the kitchen bench, or something more traditional eaten at the family table. You want to give them a treat but, whatever the menu, they'll love it because they are really there to see you.

Salmon fishcakes

If salmon is unavailable, use cod, smoked halibut or a mixture of crab and prawns to make these fishcakes. It's worth doubling the quantity and freezing the extras.

375 g skinless salmon fillets
400 g cooked mashed potatoes
3 spring onions, finely sliced
a bunch of parsley, chopped
3 eggs
100 g plain flour, plus extra for dusting
200 g breadcrumbs
300 ml sunflower oil, for frying
sea salt and freshly ground black pepper

To serve

1 lemon, cut into quarters
hollandaise sauce (see opposite)
Serves 4

Put the salmon in a medium ovenproof dish, cover with a lid and cook in a preheated oven at 350°F (180°C) Gas 4 for 10 minutes.

Remove the fish from the oven and let cool, still covered. When cool, flake the flesh with a fork.

Put the mashed potatoes in a mixing bowl. Add the flaked salmon, spring onions, parsley, salt and pepper and stir.

Beat 1 of the eggs in a small bowl with a fork, then stir it into the fish mixture.

Beat the remaining 2 eggs in the small bowl and set aside. Put the flour in a separate clean bowl and put the breadcrumbs on a plate.

Divide the fish mixture into 8 equal portions and, using floured hands, shape them into patties.

Dust each patty lightly with flour, dip it into the beaten eggs, then cover with the breadcrumbs, pressing them into the surface. Put on a large plate until needed.

Repeat until all the fish patties are coated with egg and breadcrumbs.

Heat the sunflower oil in a frying pan, add the fishcakes and cook over a medium heat until golden on both sides, approximately 5 minutes.

Serve the cooked fishcakes with lemon wedges and a jug of warm hollandaise sauce.

Hollandaise sauce

This recipe may be wicked, but to me it's the king of sauces. I think everyone should eat it once in a while and just forget about the calories. As a variation, add some finely chopped fresh herbs such as basil, chives, parsley, sage, thyme or watercress at the final moment. Note that the proper pepper to use in this instance is freshly ground white pepper, not black.

250 g butter
2 egg yolks
2 tablespoons white wine vinegar
juice of ½ lemon
sea salt and freshly ground white pepper
Serves 4

Put the butter in a small saucepan and melt it slowly over a low heat.

Put the eggs in a heatproof jug and beat with a hand-held blender. With the blender still running, pour in the melted butter in a steady stream.

Bring a large saucepan of water to the boil, then reduce the heat to low and set the jug over the water. Heat the egg mixture for 10 minutes.

Blend the mixture again (it should have thickened with the warmth), then blend in the vinegar, lemon juice, salt and pepper.

Cover with clingfilm, letting it sit on the surface of the sauce to prevent a skin forming. Leave over the pan of warm water until needed.

Baked and glazed ham

Ham is an easy dish to prepare for a large gathering and children love it. Buy a ready-boned gammon to make carving simple. A 1 kg ham will allow you some leftovers to serve cold the following week.

1 kg gammon, soaked
2 tablespoons English or Dijon mustard
2 tablespoons demerara sugar
1 teaspoon crushed cloves
freshly ground black pepper

a roasting tin, lightly oiled
Serves 4

Put the gammon in the roasting tin and cover with a sheet of kitchen foil, pleating it down the middle. Cook in a preheated oven at 160°C (325°F) Gas 3 for 1 hour.

Remove from the oven and discard the foil. Drain off the cooking juices (keep them for soups) and peel off the skin, leaving a layer of fat. Using a knife, score the fat with a criss-cross pattern.

Spread the mustard evenly over the ham. Mix the sugar, cloves and pepper in a small bowl, then sprinkle the mixture all over the ham, pressing it down into the fat with your hands.

Return the ham to the oven and bake for a further 20 minutes. Serve hot, warm or cold.

Potatoes boulangère

Finely sliced potatoes cooked in a subtle stock and allowed to dry and crisp on top: edible heaven.

1 kg floury potatoes, sliced
2 onions, finely sliced
300 ml hot chicken, beef or vegetable stock
25 g butter, finely diced
sea salt and freshly ground black pepper

a 23 cm shallow, ovenproof dish, buttered
Serves 4

Put a layer of potatoes in the buttered dish, then add a layer of onions. Season well, then repeat the layers until all the ingredients are used. Finish with a neat layer of potatoes overlapping each other and push down firmly.

Pour on the hot stock and dot the top with the butter. Bake in a preheated oven at 180°C (350°F) Gas 4 for about 1½ hours or until the top is golden brown and crunchy and the potatoes are soft right through when tested with the point of a knife.

Quick French apple tart

To make this tart sensational, do make sure the apples are sliced as finely as possible and that they are arranged neatly, 'like well-trained soldiers'.

250 g ready-made puff pastry
1 egg, beaten
4 red eating apples
30 g butter, melted
2 tablespoons soft brown sugar
½ teaspoon ground cinnamon

a baking sheet, lightly greased
Serves 4

Roll out the pastry to a rectangle measuring 30 x 18 cm. Place on the baking sheet and brush all over with the egg.

Cut the apples into quarters, removing the cores. Slice thinly and arrange in rows on top of the pastry, leaving a 5 cm gap around the edges.

Drizzle the melted butter over the apples, sprinkle with sugar and dust with cinnamon.

Brush the edges of the pastry with the remaining egg wash, then fold them inwards and gently press down.

Bake the tart in a preheated oven at 200°C (400°F) Gas 6 for 30 minutes. Reduce the heat to 180°C (350°F) Gas 4 and bake for another 15 minutes until the tart is golden all over.

Serve hot or at room temperature with clotted cream or scoops of good-quality vanilla ice cream.

Watermelon granita

On a warm summer day, this granita is cooling and very refreshing to eat. The fresh ginger gives it a subtle but delicious twist.

1 kg peeled and deseeded watermelon flesh
7 cm fresh ginger, peeled and finely diced, to serve
Serves 4

Check that all the seeds are removed from the watermelon, then put the flesh in a blender and purée until smooth.

Transfer to an ice cream machine and churn according to the manufacturer's instructions until crystallized and firm. Alternatively, place the fruit purée in a plastic box in the freezer and, every 20 minutes, remove and break up the ice crystals with a fork. Repeat at least 3 times to achieve a good, firm consistency.

When frozen, serve the watermelon granita in chilled glasses, topped with the finely diced ginger.

twilight barbecue

Outdoor entertaining is not restricted to those with a large garden or to country-dwellers. Roof terraces have become very hip in the city and, in summer, they provide a great opportunity to have friends over to watch the sun set while eating supper. This menu, with its distinctly Middle Eastern flavour, is specially designed for such an occasion.

Turkish toasted bread

Asian corner shops usually stock a wide variety of unusual and delicious items. My local has a great selection of at least eight different breads, as well as the healthiest herbs you have ever seen and it is my first choice of shop when making this recipe.

1 teaspoon harissa paste
a bunch of coriander, chopped
2 tablespoons olive oil
50 g pitted olives, chopped
2 Anaheim red chillies, deseeded and chopped
4 slices small Turkish flatbread, pita bread or small flour tortillas, separated into discs

a baking sheet
Serves 4

Put the harissa, coriander, olive oil, olives and chillies in a small bowl and mix well. Divide the mixture between the pieces of bread, then sandwich the halves back together.

Put on a baking sheet and cook in a preheated oven at 170°C (325°F) Gas 3 for 10 minutes. Remove and serve hot.

top tip: Harissa paste is a hot blend of chillies and spices available from Middle Eastern stores, delicatessens and some supermarkets. It's great to have on hand for firing up all sorts of dishes. Stir it into couscous or mix with yoghurt and serve as a dip for crudités.

Bean and mint salad

This is a great summer salad. The mix of beans and fresh mint is very refreshing and clean on the palate.

200 g broad beans, shelled and peeled
75 g peas, shelled
75 g dwarf or French beans, trimmed

top tip: Keep a spray bottle full of water near the barbecue. If the lamb's cooking juices drop into the the fire and cause any flare-ups, you can dowse the flames with a burst of spray.

75 g runner beans, sliced into 5 cm pieces
8 spring onions, trimmed and sliced
a large bunch of mint, coarsely chopped
3 tablespoons olive oil
grated zest and juice of 1 lemon
sea salt and freshly ground black pepper

Serves 4

Cook the broad beans in a large pan of boiling water for 4 minutes, then add the peas, dwarf or French beans and runner beans and continue cooking for 3 minutes. Drain, cool quickly under cold running water, then drain thoroughly.

Put the spring onions and mint in a large bowl. Add the beans, then sprinkle with the olive oil, lemon zest and juice, salt and pepper. Toss well and serve.

top tip: To turn this salad into a main course, add some crumbled feta cheese, sliced hard-boiled eggs or pieces of juicy roast ham.

Middle Eastern barbecue lamb

Butterflying means cutting the meat away from the bone to give a flatter boneless cut that vaguely resembles a butterfly. Ask your butcher to do it for you – it makes a brilliant dish that is very easy to carve at the table.

2 garlic cloves, crushed and chopped
2 teaspoons ground coriander
2 teaspoons ground cumin
2 teaspoons ground cinnamon
1 teaspoon ground ginger
2 teaspoons paprika
1–1.25 kg leg of lamb, butterflied and trimmed of fat
3 tablespoons olive oil
zest and juice of 1 lemon
sea salt

Serves 4

Put the garlic, coriander, cumin, cinnamon, ginger, paprika and salt in a large bowl and mix well. Add the lamb and rub the mixture into the meat, making sure every crevice is well coated. Drizzle with the olive oil and lemon zest and juice.

Cover and leave at room temperature for 1 hour, or in the fridge overnight. While marinating, turn the lamb over from time to time.

Light the barbecue and wait until the coals are ash-white, about 40–60 minutes. Brush the ash off the top and put the lamb on the rack.

Cook the lamb for 15–20 minutes on each side for medium rare and 30 minutes each side for well done. The exact time will vary from one barbecue to another, so if unsure, remove the lamb and carve a piece to see if it is done to your liking.

Alternatively, cook the lamb in a preheated oven at 200°C (400°F) Gas 6. For medium rare meat, put in a roasting tin and cook for 15–20 minutes, then turn, reduce the heat to 180°C (350°F) Gas 4 and cook for a further 10–15 minutes. If you prefer the meat well done, add another 10 minutes to each of these cooking times.

Preserved lemon and tomato pickle

This pickle is a great compliment to the barbecued lamb, but also goes well with cold meats such as chicken and pork. You can find Moroccan preserved lemons on sale in Middle Eastern shops, delicatessens and some of the large supermarkets.

2 tablespoons olive oil
1 onion, chopped
1 garlic clove, crushed and chopped
2-3 beef tomatoes, skinned, deseeded and
   chopped
50 g caster sugar
2 teaspoons white vinegar
a pinch of dried chilli flakes
a pinch of saffron, threads
100 g olives, pitted
1 preserved lemon, chopped
a bunch of fresh coriander, chopped

Serves 4

Heat the oil in a frying pan, add the onion and garlic and sauté for 4 minutes.

Add the tomatoes, sugar, vinegar, chilli flakes and saffron and simmer for 10 minutes until the mixture has reduced by almost half.

Add the olives, chopped preserved lemon and coriander, then remove from the heat and serve hot or cold with the lamb.

top tip: It's easy to make your own preserved lemons. Cut 4 lemons in half lengthways leaving the stalk end intact. Open the lemons up a little and place a tablespoon of salt in the middle of each one. Pack them in a preserving jar, cover with boiling water, seal and leave for two weeks in a cool dark place before using as needed.

Crusted golden rice bake

This style of rice is inspired by the method used in Persia – crunchy rice is delicious and makes a sensational change from the white and fluffy rice that we know here. If you want to make this into a meal to eat on its own, add cooked chunks of chicken to the spiced onion mixture.

200 g basmati rice
3 tablespoons olive oil
2 onions, diced
2 garlic cloves, crushed and chopped
150 g ready-to-eat dried apricots, chopped
50 g toasted sliced almonds
1 teaspoon ground turmeric
1 teaspoon crushed cardamom pods
1 tablespoon garam masala
100 g butter, cut into small pieces
sea salt and freshly ground black pepper

an ovenproof frying pan, buttered
Serves 4

Put the rice in a large bowl, wash it in several changes of cold water, then cover with cold water and let soak for 3 hours.

When ready to cook, bring a large saucepan of water to the boil. Add the rice, stir well, return to a simmer and cook for 5 minutes.

Drain the rice and fill the pan with cold water to stop it cooking any more. When cold, drain well.

Heat the olive oil in a saucepan, add the onions and garlic and cook for 5 minutes without letting it brown. Add the apricots, toasted almonds, turmeric, cardamom, garam masala and some salt and pepper and mix well.

Stir the spiced onion into the rice, then transfer it to the prepared frying pan and smooth over the top. Dot with butter and cover tightly with foil.

Cook in a preheated oven at 180°C (350°F) Gas 4 for 45 minutes, then remove the foil and cook for a further 15 minutes.

Remove from the oven, cover with a large plate and quickly invert both pan and plate. Remove the pan to reveal the rice with its golden crust.

top tip: It is worth having a good ovenproof non-stick frying pan. I use one in this recipe and to make tortilla and tarte Tatin. When buying the pan, remember the handle must be ovenproof too.

Honey and almond panna cotta

Here is a very pretty yet simple pudding you can make in advance of your party. If you don't have individual ramekins, use one large mould – a bowl will do.

1 sachet powdered gelatine, 7 g
200 ml double cream
250 g Greek yoghurt
25 g caster sugar
6 tablespoons clear honey
50 g ground almonds
1 vanilla pod, halved lengthways

4 metal or china ramekins, lightly oiled and lined with muslin or clingfilm

Serves 4

Put 3 tablespoons warm water in a small bowl, sprinkle the gelatine evenly over the top and leave until dissolved, about 5 minutes.

Put the cream in a mixing bowl. Add the yoghurt, sugar and honey and stir until smooth. Mix in the ground almonds.

Scrape the vanilla seeds out of the pod, then stir them into the cream mixture. Add the gelatine.

Pour the cream mixture into the prepared ramekins, then chill for 4 hours or until set.

To serve, turn out onto small plates. Accompany with the watermelon and rosewater salad.

Watermelon and rosewater salad

Refreshing and easy is the best description of this attractive salad. Watermelons are a special Middle Eastern delicacy, so if you have a specialist shop near you, try buying your watermelon there.

1 small watermelon, about 1.5 kg, chilled
2 tablespoons rosewater

Rose petals
8–12 unsprayed pink rose petals
1 egg white, beaten
1 tablespoon caster sugar

Serves 4

To prepare the rose petals, dip them in the beaten egg white, then lightly dust with caster sugar, and set aside to dry for 1 hour.

Top and tail the watermelon, then slice it into thin wedges and pick out the seeds.

Arrange on a large serving plate, sprinkle with the rosewater, cover and chill. Serve decorated with the sugar-dusted rose petals.

top tip: When you are buying a watermelon, choose one that has a tight and unblemished skin. Tap on it with your knuckles – it should make a solid noise, and definitely not sound hollow.

dinner party dream

Is it a birthday, anniversary, or time to celebrate a well-deserved promotion at work? Treat your friends to the best you can offer with this stunning, thoroughly grown-up dinner party. There is no need to feel on a knife edge when preparing special occasion food – these inspirational menus are carefully conceived to create maximum impact with minimum fuss. Pour the champagne and prepare to dazzle...

However relaxed our lives, we all aspire now and then to give a stylish, elegant dinner party with a sensational menu, beautiful matching china and cutlery, exquisite napkins, swathes of flowers, glowing candles, fine wines and laughing guests. This is all possible, no matter how busy you may feel. Even simply dressed tables can look absolutely gorgeous and I am sure that the spirit of the occasion helps to bring our kitchen skills alive.

There are a few key tricks you can use to plan easy dinner party menus. Make sure that one course, ideally the starter, needs only very simple, brief cooking – a salad or my gingered asparagus with cashew nuts is ideal. Then pick a pudding that can be made well in advance and stored, one that if not cold, only requires a small amount of cooking to finish it off. This frees your mind and time to concentrate on the hot main dish, but even so, choose something simple and stunning that allows you to relax and enjoy your own party – an impressive steamed fish with Thai flavours is perfect.

Ginger asparagus with cashews

Fresh asparagus stir-fried with ginger, orange, soy sauce and cashew nuts, then finished with a drizzle of sesame oil makes a very simple starter to grace the table.

1 tablespoon peanut oil
375 g asparagus, halved lengthways
1.5 cm fresh ginger, peeled and cut into fine matchsticks
75 g roasted cashew nuts, chopped
grated zest of 1 orange
1 tablespoon soy sauce
1 tablespoon sesame oil
Serves 4

Heat the peanut oil in a wok, add the asparagus and ginger and stir-fry for 4 minutes.

Add the cashews, orange zest, soy sauce and sesame oil and continue cooking for 1 minute. Transfer to plates and serve immediately.

Spanish roast pepper salad

Mahon is sold in many supermarkets.

8 red peppers, halved, cored and deseeded
4 tablespoons olive oil
100 g Mahon cheese, or other hard cheese
100 g pitted black olives
a bunch of flat leaf parsley, chopped
1 tablespoon white wine vinegar
sea salt and freshly ground black pepper
fresh crusty bread, warmed, to serve

a baking sheet, lightly oiled
Serves 4

Place the peppers on the lightly oiled baking sheet, drizzle with the olive oil and roast in a preheated oven at 180°C (350°F) Gas 4 for 15-20 minutes or until the peppers are soft.

Slice the cheese as finely as possible (a truffle slicer makes this easy). In a salad bowl, combine the cheese, peppers, olives, parsley, vinegar and seasoning. Serve with warm crusty bread.

Steamed sea bass with Thai soup

Sea bass is a beautiful but pricey fish and I admit it's not always available. However, you can substitute it in this recipe with cod fillets, halibut or tuna steaks, or tiger prawns. Remember to ask the fishmonger for some bones to make the fish stock.

4 sea bass, 500 g each, filleted with bones reserved
1 white onion, sliced
1 stalk lemongrass, chopped
2.5 cm fresh ginger, sliced
a large bunch of coriander, leaves chopped and roots or stalks kept separately
2 garlic cloves, sliced
1 fresh red or green chilli, chopped
1 kaffir lime leaf or a strip of lime rind
1 tablespoon soy sauce
100 g mushrooms, sliced
4 spring onions, sliced into rounds
leaves from a bunch of basil, torn
400 g udon noodles
extra coriander leaves, to garnish

a 2-tier saucepan with steamer
Serves 4

Put the fish bones in a medium saucepan. Add 1.2 litres water, the onion, lemongrass, ginger, coriander roots or stalks, garlic, chilli, lime leaf or rind, and soy sauce. Bring to the boil, then reduce the heat and simmer for 15 minutes, skimming the scum regularly.

When the stock is cooked, strain several times through muslin or a fine sieve.

Arrange the steamer, putting the fish stock in the lower section. Fold the fish fillets in half, pinning them with a cocktail stick if needed, then place in the steamer section. Set over a moderately high heat and steam for 4 minutes.

Remove from the heat and lift the steamer section from the top of the pan. Add the mushrooms,

spring onions, coriander leaves, basil and noodles to the fish stock and stir. Re-assemble the steamer and continue steaming for 5 minutes more.

Serve the noodle soup in large bowls topped with the steamed sea bass and sprinkled with the extra coriander leaves.

Chicken with chestnuts and Puy lentils

Puy lentils come from the Velay region of France and have an excellent flavour that works particularly well in this recipe. All the flavours stay in the pan to give a rich dish.

5 tablespoons olive oil
4 shallots, diced
2 onions, sliced
2 garlic cloves, crushed and chopped
100 g chicken livers, trimmed and chopped
125 g peeled chestnuts, chopped
100 g Puy lentils, soaked in water for 1 hour
grated zest and juice of 1 lemon
1 bayleaf
a sprig of thyme
4 chicken breasts on the bone, unskinned
1 tablespoon plain flour
300 ml chicken stock
100 ml red wine
50 g butter
1 pear, cored and sliced
sea salt and freshly ground black pepper
a bunch of flat leaf parsley, chopped

a shallow ovenproof dish or roasting tin
Serves 4

Heat half the olive oil in a saucepan. Add the shallots, onions and garlic and cook over a low heat for 6 minutes, stirring frequently.

Add the chicken livers and cook for 2 minutes. Then add the chopped chestnuts, lentils, lemon zest and juice, bayleaf and thyme, mix well and cook for a further 3 minutes.

Transfer the mixture to a shallow ovenproof dish or roasting tin and set aside.

Heat the remaining olive oil in the saucepan, add the chicken and sauté gently until golden brown. Place on top of the mixture in the roasting tin.

Add the flour to the saucepan and mix well to form a paste with the pan juices. Slowly add the chicken stock and mix to give a smooth sauce.

Stir in the wine and some salt and pepper, then bring to the boil and cook for 2 minutes.

Pour the sauce into the roasting tin and cover with foil. Cook in a preheated oven at 200°C (400°F) Gas 6 for 20 minutes. Remove the foil and return to the oven until the chicken is brown (add more stock if needed to moisten the lentils).

Melt the butter in a frying pan, add the sliced pear and fry gently until golden. Add the parsley and spoon the mixture over the chicken and lentils just before serving on a large platter.

menu 1

Ginger asparagus with cashews

Steamed sea bass with Thai soup

Chilled lemon soufflés

Sauvignon Blanc

menu 2

Spanish roast pepper salad

Chicken with chestnuts and Puy lentils

Sautéed vegetables in shallot butter

Plum clafoutis

Sparkling Shiraz

Sautéed vegetables in shallot butter

Baby vegetables can be used for this recipe if you are short of time and feeling rich.

100 g parsnips, cut into 5 cm pieces
100 g carrots, cut into 5 cm pieces
100 g butter
4 shallots, diced
100 g leeks, cut into 5 cm pieces
100 g courgettes, cut into 5 cm pieces
100 g sugarsnap peas, trimmed
100 g mushrooms, halved if large
100 g runner beans, cut into 5 cm pieces
sea salt and freshly ground black pepper
a bunch of chervil, chopped, to serve

Serves 4

Bring a saucepan of water to the boil, add the carrots and parsnips, simmer for 10 minutes, then drain well.

Melt the butter in a large frying pan, add the shallots and cook for 5 minutes over a low heat without letting them brown.

Add all the trimmed vegetables and sauté for 6 minutes. Just before serving, add salt, pepper and chopped chervil and toss well so tht all the vegetables are coated with the flavoured butter.

Chilled lemon soufflés

This citrus soufflé is a light, refreshing end to a meal and great to serve at parties as it can be made in advance. Bear in mind that

uncooked eggs should not be consumed by pregnant women or the elderly.

2 tablespoons powdered gelatine
grated zest and juice of 3 lemons
3 eggs, separated
75 g caster sugar
150 ml double cream
60 g mixture of dark and white chocolate, shaved or grated

a 1 litre soufflé dish, wrapped with a paper cuff to a height of 5 cm above the rim and secured with string

Serves 4

Place 3 tablespoons hot water in a heatproof bowl, then sprinkle in the gelatine. Leave to stand until the gelatine dissolves, then place in saucepan of water and heat gently until the gelatine dissolves completely.

Put the lemon zest, juice, egg yolks and sugar in a large bowl and beat with an electric whisk.

When the gelatine has dissolved, pour it slowly into the egg mixture, whisking constantly.

In a large bowl, whisk the cream to soft peaks.

Place the egg whites in another large bowl and whisk until stiff. Fold in the lemon mixture and whipped cream until smoothly blended.

Spoon the soufflé mixture into the prepared dish and chill for at least 2 hours or until set.

When set, shave or grate the chocolates directly onto the surface of the soufflé so that the curls are piled high. Carefully remove the paper cuff and keep the soufflé chilled until ready to serve.

Plum clafoutis

For a very decadent pudding, use single cream instead of milk in this recipe. You can also use other stone fruits or berries.

750 g plums, halved and stoned
4 eggs
500 ml milk
75g plain flour
75 g caster sugar
1 tablespoon icing sugar
pouring cream, to serve

a shallow ovenproof dish, 25 cm square, lightly buttered

Serves 4

Arrange the halved plums in the buttered dish. Beat the eggs in a jug, add the milk and mix well.

Sift the flour into a medium bowl, add the sugar and make a well in the centre. Slowly whisk in the milk mixture until it is all incorporated and the batter is smooth and glossy.

Pour the batter over the plums and bake in a preheated oven at 190°C (375°F) Gas 5 for 40 minutes or until golden and firm to touch.

Lightly dust the clafoutis with the icing sugar before serving with cream.

dinner date

Oh, what sweetness a romantic meal can be. Food and love really do go hand in hand. Everyone can remember a meal enjoyed with their beloved – the place, food, flowers, wine, music and words all seem more vivid when your companion is a special someone. Set the date, treat yourself to a new outfit and plan an evening to make your love bloom.

Any day can be Valentine's Day when you make the effort to charm your sweetheart. We are all so busy that sometimes the most important person is forgotten, so make time to sit down, eat a meal together and look dreamily into each other's eyes while you whisper sweet nothings.

Lay the table with romance in mind, using vibrant shades of reds and pinks. Fill the room with fragrant flowers and decadently scatter the floor with petals. Light candles and tea

lights, open the wine and cook your meal. Don't answer the phone or door, just enjoy each other in your cosy nest.

Keep the menu short – this is precisely the evening you do not want to feel as though you have eaten too much – but pay special attention to the presentation of your meal. This exotic feast is ideal for your dinner a deux: aromatic marinated Chinese duck followed by lightly poached pears cooked with star anise and drizzled with chocolate – very saucy.

Chinese duck breast

Begin marinating the duck breasts the day before your intended liaison. This allows the ingredients to mingle and add their lovely flavours to the meat.

4 duck breasts, skin removed
4 tablespoons vegetable oil
3 red peppers, sliced into thin strips
1 large onion, sliced
1 chilli, cored and chopped
100 g cooked rice
2 teaspoons caster sugar
250 g baby spinach, shredded
a bunch of chives, chopped

Lemon-soy marinade
juice of 1 lemon
4 tablespoons honey
3 tablespoons dark soy sauce
2 tablespoons olive oil
2 garlic cloves, crushed and chopped
freshly ground black pepper
Serves 4

To marinate the duck breasts, put the lemon juice, honey, soy sauce, olive oil, garlic and some freshly ground pepper in a large bowl. Add the duck breasts and turn to coat with the marinade.

Cover and chill overnight, turning as often as possible. Remove the duck, shaking off any excess marinade and reserve the remainde.

Heat half the vegteable oil in a frying pan. Add the duck. Cook over a high heat for 5 minutes on each side, then reduce the heat to low and fry for a further 5 minutes on each side. Remove from the heat and let rest in the pan to set the juices.

Heat the remaining 2 tablespoons vegetable oil in a wok. Add the peppers, onion and chilli and stir-fry for 5 minutes. Add the cooked rice, mix well and cook for a further 5 minutes.

Sprinkle in the sugar, shredded spinach and half the chives. Cook for 3 minutes until the spinach has just wilted.

Meanwhile, slice the duck breasts and pour the juices into a small saucepan. Add the reserved marinade and bring to the boil.

Spoon the rice onto warm plates, arrange the duck on top. Spoon over the sauce and sprinkle with the ramaining chives.

menu

Chinese duck breast

Pears with star anise and
chocolate drizzle

Gewürztraminer

Pears with star anise and chocolate drizzle

Chocolate sauce is so easy to make and compliments pears fantastically. This dish looks stunning and can be prepared in advance, then simply assembled when needed – just keep the chocolate sauce warm and leave the pears in the warm wine.

4 ripe pears, peeled
200 ml white wine
4 star anise
50 g sugar
75 g dark chocolate (70 per cent cocoa solids)
75 ml double cream

Serves 4

Put the pears in a saucepan, pour over the wine, add the star anise and sugar and bring to the boil. Reduce the heat, cover and simmer for 10 minutes. Turn off the heat and let the pears steep in the liquid for 1 hour, still covered.

Fill a small saucepan with water and heat to simmering point. Place the chocolate in a heatproof bowl that fits snugly over the saucepan. Turn the heat down, set the bowl over the water and leave the chocolate to melt. Add the cream and mix to make a smooth, glossy sauce.

Serve the pears warm or cold, drizzled with the sauce.

Cravings have a tendency to strike late at night, especially after a maybe-too-riotous evening out. On these occasions, homely hot snacks are the best way to bring satisfaction. Who can resist melted cheese on toast, made with a good tasty mature Cheddar and splashed with Worcestershire sauce? Or creamy scrambled eggs with buttery sautéed mushrooms? With these scrumptious recipes you may never phone for takeaway again.

Cheese on toast

This is a great snack, especially when served on a big bed of salad including avocado, cucumber, lettuce, tomatoes, sliced red onion and herbs, all tossed in olive oil, salt and pepper. I call this a 'fridge salad' because, however low the supplies of fresh food are in our house, you can usually find most of the above ingredients.

4 slices bread
200 g mature Cheddar cheese, sliced
Worcestershire sauce, to taste
sea salt and freshly ground black pepper
Serves 4

Toast the bread in a toaster or under a hot grill. Arrange the slices of cheese on top of the toast, making sure it hangs slightly over the edges.

Grill for 8-10 minutes, or until the cheese is bubbling and golden. Serve sprinkled with Worcestershire sauce, salt and pepper.

Farmhouse sauté with bacon and onions

A good high-starch, late-night feast. You could also add some tomatoes cut into generous chunks – don't cook them, just let them cool with the potatoes and serve with a dash of balsamic vinegar. This dish is also fabulous served at a barbecue.

3 tablespoons olive oil
1 kg cooked potatoes, thickly sliced
2 onions, diced
175 g bacon, chopped
3 sprigs of thyme
sea salt and freshly ground black pepper
Serves 4

Heat the olive oil in a large frying pan over a medium heat. Add the sliced cooked potatoes and fry on each side until golden. Remove the potatoes with a slotted spoon and set aside to drain on kitchen paper.

Add the onion, bacon and thyme to the frying pan and cook over a medium heat, stirring constantly, until the mixture is crisp and golden.

Add the cooked potatoes and salt and pepper to taste. Mix well and serve at once.

late night feast

Mushrooms on toast with scrambled eggs

These days there are so many different types of mushroom available. For this dish, try buying large open flat mushrooms; they make this simple snack look sensational.

125 g butter, plus extra for spreading
4 large open mushrooms
6 eggs, beaten
4 slices bread
sea salt and freshly ground black pepper
Serves 4

Melt 25 g of the butter in a large frying pan. Add the mushrooms and cook over a medium heat for 5 minutes on each side.

In a separate non-stick saucepan, melt 50 g of the butter until foaming, then pour in the beaten eggs.

Using a wooden spoon, stir the eggs well until the mixture is just starting to set. Remove from the heat immediately and season to taste with the salt and pepper.

Cut the remaining butter into small pieces and add it to the eggs, mixing well until combined.

Toast the bread and spread lightly with butter. Cut in half diagonally, top with the scrambled egg and mushrooms and serve at once.

French toast and fried tomatoes

Children love French toast, which is also sometimes called eggy bread. Topping it with fried tomatoes makes a juicy, tasty snack. Frying tomatoes seems to intensify their flavour and the heat makes them soft and velvety – truly delicious on eggy bread.

4 eggs
4 tablespoons milk
4 slices bread
50 g butter
4 ripe or green tomatoes, halved
sea salt and freshly ground black pepper
Serves 4

Beat together the eggs, milk and some salt and pepper in a large, shallow dish. Add the bread and leave to soak for 5 minutes on each side so that all the egg mixture is absorbed.

Heat a large, non-stick frying pan over a medium heat. Add the soaked bread and cook over a medium-low heat for 3-4 minutes on each side.

In a separate frying pan, melt the butter. Add the tomatoes and fry on each side for 2 minutes, then serve on top of the hot French toast.

No matter whether you are curled up with your loved one in front of the television, or working late at home to meet a deadline, a warm and thoughtfully cooked morsel is the most gratifying treat. Keep it simple and savoury.

back to basics

Good cooking is easy when you follow a few simple rules. Here are sound kitchen tips you'll want to make second nature, plus advice on shopping and keeping key ingredients, and a few easy things you can do right now to enhance your food.

Let's start simply: every kitchen needs one sharp knife, a chopping board and a saucepan, then I am smiling. These are my three basic 'must-haves' to cook any meal.

Cheese

Buy cheese from speciality cheese shops, where they are knowledgeable and can help you make the correct decision. It is important to know when you will be eating the cheese, so that you can buy a perfectly ripe one for your table.

Buying fish and seafood

Fish and seafood should come from a busy shop and have a clean, fresh smell. The fish eyes should be plump and clear, the scales regular and in place and the flesh should be firm, clean and bright in colour. Prawns should be firm and evenly coloured. Molluscs should be closed or, if open, they should quickly shut when tapped on the kitchen bench. Never accept second best – go to another shop or choose another recipe.

Meat should look bright and full of moisture. The fat should be evenly marbled throughout but there should not be an excess. Poultry should have a slightly moist skin and a clean smell. Never buy anything that looks dull and dry, it is not good enough for your kitchen.

Check 'use by' dates on store cupboard food as things do loose their zing, for example spices, herbs, dried and canned pulses and so on. Either use them up quickly or discard.

Always buy quality, not quantity
Honestly, you will taste the difference and enjoy the pleasure it brings. When shopping, select the freshest and best looking food available. If what you require for a certain recipe is not good enough, use something else or cook something else. Don't accept poor produce – it will make your cooking poor too, and that style does not exist in my books!

Stove-top grill pans
If using a stove-top grill pan, always heat it over a high heat so the pan gets really hot before adding any food. This will give you the perfect result. Also, don't fiddle with pan-grilled food while it's cooking – leave it to seal on one side and get a good crust and ridged effect, then flip it over and repeat the no-fiddle treatment.

Wherever possible, use fresh **herbs**. Chop them just before use and add with abundance. Flat leaf parsley should be given a knighthood...I love it. Add it to pasta, fish, beans, casseroles, soups, new potatoes, salads – the list is endless.

Knives
For perfect chopping and slicing, use a wet stone to sharpen your knives, and use it frequently.

Never serve food (except the obvious, ice cream, ice etc.) fridge-cold. You can't taste it. Instead, allow it to sit in the kitchen for 30 minutes or more until it reaches room temperature to wake up the flavours.

Be passionate about your kitchen and what goes in it, then your food will improve.....honestly.

To avoid a hot, greasy and unmanageable mess, always use chilled butter when making pastry.

The best dressed salad in town

Take a good selection of your favourite leaves, break them up and place in a large bowl. Add 2 tablespoons of the very best extra virgin olive oil, the juice of a lemon, some sea salt and freshly ground black pepper, then roll up your sleeves and toss the salad with your hands for 3-4 minutes until every leaf is glistening and thinly coated with the dressing.

Stock is easy to make. The best ones usually contain bones, onion, celery, carrot, leek, garlic, bay leaf, salt and pepper. Cover with water, bring to the boil and simmer for 20 minutes (fish stock) or 1 hour (meat stock). Strain and allow to cool. When cold, skim any fat from the top (it will have set on the surface) and freeze the stock until needed. The more jellied your stock, the better the flavour will be. Use it in a risotto or soup and it will taste fantastic.

Be sure to wear an apron in the kitchen, as good cooks will use their hands.

Steam cuisine

Be kind to your green vegetables and do not overcook them – they will taste much better and look brighter for it. Try steaming vegetables and you will find the difference in taste and texture is wonderful. I am a steamaholic.

Keep a selection of oils in the cupboard

You need a good extra virgin olive oil for salads and drizzling. Sesame, pumpkin, walnut and infused oils can be used like condiments to add flavour to salads and hot dishes.

For cooking, keep a pure olive oil for Mediterranean-style foods, plus some sunflower or vegetable oil for those dishes (such as stir-fries) that should not take on the flavour of the oil.

Buy a good quality pepper mill and use it regularly. I always use freshly ground black pepper in my cooking, it has the best flavour.

Onions are an important kitchen ingredient, but never frizzle and brown them when mixing them with other foods – it will ruin the texture and give a disappointing flavour.

Ovens and stoves

Gas hobs are without a doubt my favourite for cooking because the flame can be adjusted instantly. However I prefer to use an electric fan-assisted oven for roasting and baking as I think they cook more evenly than other ovens. If you are shopping for new kitchen gear, my advice is to buy a gas hob and a fan-assisted electric oven.

Vanilla sugar gives a lovely flavour to puddings, custards and cakes. Fill a kilner jar with caster sugar and chop a couple of vanilla pods into 5 cm lengths. Add them to the sugar, mix through, and leave to infuse for a week or so before use in your favourite sweet dishes.

To make your own **mint sauce**, chop lots of fresh mint, add a teaspoon of caster sugar and cover with some white wine vinegar. Allow to steep for at least an hour before serving alongside simply roasted lamb.

Crushing garlic

To crush garlic really well, first smash the whole clove with the flat of a large knife. Hold it flat against the garlic and press down using your weight. Peel and chop the clove, then add $\frac{1}{2}$ teaspoon salt and mash the garlic with the flat part of your knife blade.

index

spinach and bacon salad with Dijon
dressing, 112
the Works, 21
espresso granita, 64

F

family picnic, 51–6
family Saturday lunch, 76–7
farmhouse sauté with bacon and onions,
179
fennel, mozzarella cheese with new
potatoes and, 69
feta, onion and cucumber salad, 75
finger food, 136–41
fish, 182
bouillabaisse, 129
fish stock, 129
menu planner, 13
fishcakes, salmon, 152–3
flapjacks, 27
focaccia with grilled chicken, 96
French 75, 138
French apple tart, 154
French beans: bean and mint salad, 158–9
green bean and herb broth, 131
salad Niçoise, 122
French toast: French toast and fried
tomatoes, 180
panettone French toast, 37
fruit: damper with red berry salad, 48
fruit platter, 31
Swiss muesli, 21
see also individual types of fruit
fruit cake, celebration iced, 108–10

G

gammon: baked and glazed ham, 153
garden lunch, 57–65
garlic: crushing, 185
garlic bread, 76
garlic toast, 47
leg of lamb with rosemary and garlic, 80
gazpacho soup, 87
gin: French 75, 138
ginger: ginger asparagus with cashews,
166
lemon and ginger infusion, 107
still ginger lemonade, 53

goats' cheese: goats' cheese and pepper
crostini, 141
tomato and goats' cheese tart, 93
granita: espresso granita, 64
watermelon granita, 155
granola, house, 17
grapes: white wine spritzer, 50
green bean and herb broth, 131
green chicken curry, 151
green tea, 18
griddling, 183

H

haddock *see* smoked haddock
ham: baked and glazed ham, 153
cheesy stuffed croissants, 87
thyme and ham tortilla, 96
mountain eggs, 100
roasted butternut, tomato and Parma
ham salad, 73
herbs, 183
herbal teas, 18
leaf and herb salad, 59
herring roe: Avruga baby baked potatoes,
137
hobs, 185
hollandaise sauce, 153
honey: honey and almond panna cotta,
162
honey yoghurt, 31
hoummus and salad in Turkish flatbread,
95
house granola, 17

I

iced jasmine tea, 107
ices: espresso granita, 64
watermelon granita, 155

J

jam biscuits, coconut, 109
jasmine tea, iced, 107

K

kedgeree with poached eggs, 35
kick-starter Bloody Mary, 29
knives, 183
kumquats: lobby dazzler, 142

L

lamb: leg of lamb with rosemary and garlic,
80
Middle Eastern barbecue lamb, 159
roasting times, 79
leaf and herb salad, 59
leeks: artichoke and cheese tart, 146
vegetable noodle stir-fry, 133
lemon: chilled lemon soufflés, 168
French 75, 138
lemon and ginger infusion, 107
lemon meringue pie, 84
lemon spaghetti, 112
lemon syrup cake, 108
lemon tart, 75
preserved lemon and tomato pickle, 161
rosemary and lemon roasted chicken, 58
still ginger lemonade, 53
lentils: chicken with chestnuts and Puy
lentils, 167
curried lentils and spinach, 119
warm Mediterranean Puy lentil salad, 70
lettuce: chicken liver salad, 72
hoummus and salad in Turkish flatbread,
95
peppered beef with watercress salad,
146
salad Niçoise, 122
lime: mojito, 141
liver: chicken liver salad, 72
lobby dazzler, 142
lunches: classic Sunday roast, 78–85
garden lunch, 57–65
Saturday family lunch, 76–7
winter lunch, 74–5
working lunch, 86–91

M

mangetout: summer beans and couscous
salad, 66
martinis: blueberry martini, 137
brazen martini, 137
marzipan: celebration iced fruit cake,
108–10
mascarpone cheese, tiramisu, 148
meat, 182
menu planner, 13
roasting times, 79

acknowledgements

The publisher and author would like to thank the following companies and stores who loaned glassware, plates, bowls, cutlery, table linen and accessories that appear in the book:

Bodanova
Unit F4
Kingsway Buisness Park
Oldfield Park
Hampton
TW12 2HD
020 8979 2929 for stockists

Bridgewater
739 Fulham Road
London
SW6 5UL
020 7371 5264 for mail order catalogue
and stores

The Conran Shop
81 Fulham Road
London
SW3 6RD
020 7589 7401 for stores

David Mellor
4 Sloane Square
London
SW1W 8EE
020 7730 4259 for mail order catalogue
and stores

Designers Guild Store
267–271 and 275–277 Kings Road
London
SW3 58N
020 7243 7300

General Trading Company
144 Sloane Street
London
SW1X 9BL
020 7730 0411

Habitat UK
196 Tottenham Court
London
W1P 9ID
0845 6010 740 for store details

Haveli Designs Limited
81 Loudoun Road
London
NW8 0DQ
020 7328 8535 for mail order catalogue

Home Place
26–34 Kensington High Street
London
W8 4PF
020 7937 2626

House
P.O. Box 1748
Salisbury
SP5 5SP
01725 552549 for mail order catalogue
and stores

Lakeland Ltd
Alexandra Building
Windermere
Cumbria
LA23 1BQ
01539 488100 for mail order catalogue
and stores

Monsoon Home
33C Kings Road
London
SW3 4LX
020 7313 3000 for stores

Muji
167–169 Great Portland Street
London
W1N 5FD
020 7323 2287
020 7323 2208 for store details

Sodahl Design
59 New Concordia Wharf
Mill Street
London
SE1 2BB
020 7237 6561

Urban Outfitters
36–38 Kensington High Street
London
W8 4PF
020 7761 1000

Thanks also to OneAldwich, One Aldwich, London, WC2B 4BZ, for supplying the cocktail recipes on pages 137–142 and for allowing us to photograph at the bar. To Ginkco Garden Centre, Ravenscourt Park, London, thanks for donating the plants and flowers that appear in the book. Finally a big thank you to the staff at Priory Bay Hotel, Priory Drive, Seaview, Isle of Wight, UK (01983 613146) for all their assistance.